December 2001

For Lupine~

It's like porno for

bibliophiles!

Enjoy!

Christine ♡

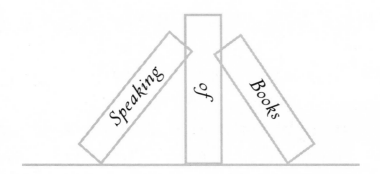

Also by the Authors

A PASSION FOR BOOKS:

A Book Lover's Treasury of Stories,
Essays, Humor, Lore, and Lists on Collecting, Reading,
Borrowing, Lending, Caring for, and Appreciating Books

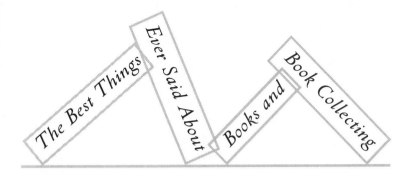

The Best Things Ever Said About Books and Book Collecting

Speaking of Books

Edited by

ROB KAPLAN *and* HAROLD RABINOWITZ

 Crown Publishers / New York

Published by
Crown Publishers,
New York, New York.
Member of the Crown
Publishing Group.

Random House, Inc.
New York, Toronto,
London, Sydney, Auckland
www.randomhouse.com

CROWN is a trademark
and the Crown colophon is
a registered trademark of
Random House, Inc.

Printed in the United States
of America

DESIGN BY
BARBARA STURMAN

Library of Congress
Cataloging-in-Publication
Data
    Speaking of books : the
best things ever said about
books and book collecting
/ edited by Rob Kaplan
and Harold Rabinowitz.
—1st ed.
Includes index.
    1. Books—Quotations,
maxims, etc.   2. Book
collecting—Quotations,
maxims, etc.   I. Kaplan,
Rob.   II. Rabinowitz,
Harold, 1948–.
PN6084.B65 S67   2001
002—dc21   00-065585

ISBN 0-609-60852-5

10 9 8 7 6 5 4 3 2 1

First Edition

Grateful acknowledgment is
made to the following for
permission to reprint previ-
ously published material:

FABER AND FABER: Excerpts
from *The Anatomy of
Bibliomania* by Holbrook
Jackson. Reprinted by permission of Faber and Faber.

ROGER ROSENBLATT
AND THE WATKINS/
LOOMIS AGENCY:
Excerpts from *Bibliomania* by
Roger Rosenblatt. Reprinted
by permission of Roger
Rosenblatt and the
Watkins/Loomis Agency.

To my parents,
Herbert and Evelyn Kaplan,
who so many years ago instilled in me
a love of reading and books

RAK

To Isadore Serot, of blessed memory,
who loved his people, his family,
and the world of learning

HR

Contents

Introduction: Books in Our Future / ix

1. In Praise of Books / 3

2. The Pleasures of Buying and Owning Books / 17

3. What to Read / 29

4. The Influence of Books / 45

5. Bibliomania / 57

6. The Pleasures of Reading / 67

7. What Books Do—and Don't Do—for Us / 81

8. All Those Books . . . / 97

9. How to Read / 105

10. Libraries / 113

11. Good Books and Bad / 125

12. The Comfort Found in Books / 139

13. Lending and Borrowing Books / 151

14. Books and the Young / 161

15. What Books Can—and Cannot—Teach Us / 169

16. Authors and Their Readers / 183

17. Collectors and Collecting / 195

18. The Book Trade / 207

19. The Enemies of Books / 217

20. Books Forever! / 227

Index of Authors / 245

Introduction: Books in Our Future

IN OUR PREVIOUS EFFORT, *A Passion for Books,* we
collected essays, stories, memoirs, lists, a map of New
York City's Fourth Avenue bookstores from the early
1950s, and even a few *New Yorker*–style cartoons relating
to books. We were celebrating the love of books, pure
and simple, and there didn't seem to be any need for a
justification of what we were doing. Books have played
so central and vital a role in the development of our
culture, so pivotal a role in our lives, that it would seem
ungrateful and mean-spirited not to simply acknowledge
those debts with a collection such as ours. If there was
any sense that something was awry, that there was
something book-lovers had to be worried about
threatening the future of books, we set it aside and went
about our business. One of us proposed an introduction
to the first work that was fairly hysterical, chastising
the pooh-bahs of the electronic media for thinking for
a moment they were mounting a serious challenge to
the importance and centrality of books in the culture.
But after a collaborative slap in the face and a dowsing

with an editorial bucket of cold water, cooler heads
prevailed and the introduction was bright and cheery—
and befitting the celebratory tone we were trying
to achieve.

During the course of our collaboration, we discovered
other passions we share. We both collect and admire
aphorisms—those brief statements of judgment or
value that capture wisdom in their cadence, that convey
authority in their syntax. We realize that this is an odd
taste, perhaps an acquired one. Why, after all, should
some assertion be believed simply because it was said
with a flourish or put very well? Does that make it true?
There are probably quotable lines in works espousing
philosophies we would abhor, felicitous turns of phrase
promoting ideas and values we would find repugnant.
Why make so much out of the elegance of something
somebody said? Doesn't it cheapen the substance of the
work in which the quotation is embedded? Take one
line out of Plato to admire it and it seems you are
dismissing all the crystalline reasoning (and hard work)
that went into the rest of the dialogue.

But there may be something more to it than that.
At times, while reading, you may have felt the presence
of the author coming to you through the words. At such
times it seems the author is standing right there, and
you are flushed with a sense of recognition—you believe
you would *know* this person if the two of you ever met.
Perhaps it is an illusion—we might well be disappointed

if we met the author and found a character wholly different from our expectations. It's been known to happen. In the recent movie *As Good as It Gets,* a writer of romance novels is depicted as a despicable character, a bigot who throws little dogs down the incinerator chute in his luxury New York apartment building. Could this man's horrid character really not infect his writing? We don't think so. (This is only a movie.) Writing is self-revelatory whether or not the writer wants to be revealed. Authors as well as characters have a way of becoming real to the reader.

If we are familiar with an author's work, we imagine him or her speaking to us, and feel an intimacy with the author through the words on the paper. It's the sense we have of the writer that makes us seek out other works by the same author; it's what allows writers to get away with writing the same book over and over again. Because we felt the presence of the writer coming through in the first book, having enjoyed the writer's company during that reading, we decide to entertain another visit from an old friend. This mystical quality of writing has been noticed since the beginning of recorded history—it's part of the sanctity of the Scriptures and the flame that burns through the epics of Homer; it's what makes Shakespeare so enduring and Thurber so much fun to read today. Somewhere in the pages that follow, Jorge Luis Borges has it that writers become their books when they die. We think this happens much sooner.

And this is the quality that characterizes the

aphorism. When the remark is connected to its author, we can feel the presence of the author. Something about the way the phrase is put together contains the presence of the author, and that's what we are responding to. One of us recently lost a relative who was fond of saying, "You don't have to see *Snow White and the Seven Dwarfs* a hundred times to know how it ends." What is so poignant about this quote is not simply the wisdom contained within it. There's a presence that shines through it. Those who knew the man can still hear him saying it; those who did not can get a glimpse, a hint, of the kind of person he was. In the same way, aphorisms tell us about their authors.

But this is an age in which the aphorism is in low ebb. Not simply because we are bereft of wise men (or wise guys), but because we are isolated from one another and isolated within our own worlds. When we forget the pleasure of personal contact with friends and family, and in social communion, those artifacts that invoke sensations of personal contact depreciate. But for those of us still sensitive to it, the pleasure we get from a well-wrought aphorism is uncanny.

While we may bemoan the decline of the aphorism in our culture—perhaps acknowledging how easily a phrase can manipulate, thereby making all artfully phrased sentiments suspect—and agree to present this collection to the aficionados who still appreciate the aphoristic art, we're not going to sit still and watch while books, too, make the endangered species list, are we?

During the preparation of our first volume, the electronic book was just a gleam in some people's eyes, electronic publishing a distant rumble on the horizon. Now the major publishers have founded divisions with mandates to exploit this medium. As you read this, these enterprises are well under way. Publishers offer electronic books online to be read on computer screens, but not necessarily on the CRT displays that grace most desks in business today. The observation that these are difficult conveyances of information is already commonplace, and no one (in his right mind) believes reading long tracts of material in such circumstances will replace or even challenge books.

But will the book as it has been known and loved become obsolete? What is its place in this vision of the future of written communication? Can it live alongside the electronic book taken to its logical and technological extension: something with a rectangular screen the size of a page, capable of print-quality resolution, fed new text (and enhanced with audio and video) through a wireless connection to a virtually limitless information base? New technologies may force us to change our very definition of that thing called a book, or perhaps that handy letter "e" will continue to signify what we feel is a crucial distinction between one kind of book and the other. Surely the new technology will alter relationships between authors, readers, and publishers; between the person and the page; between words and life. We fear that the opportunity, even the desire, for a person to "curl up with a good book"—and the values and quality of life that represents—may be threatened by the inhuman pace and socioeconomics of the so-called information age. The literacy problem isn't just that there are too many people who don't know how to read, the problem is that there are too many people without the requisite patience to endure an entire book!

However, we should not—and will not—be dismissed as technophobes. We use the Internet, PDAs, electronic databases, and many different computer applications as we edit and produce books for different publishers in consultation with authors around the globe. We do our part to forge this brave new world of publishing. We create material that will find its way onto the Internet, and material expressly for Internet use—and make no apologies for it. Still, we love our books. Some actors work on the stage, some in the movies, and some on TV. The particular advantages, limitations, and demands of each medium as it evolves may require corresponding changes in the craft, but a robust medium will not be supplanted by another. Movies do not substitute for the thrill and artistry of live theater, and television hasn't emptied the movie houses.

So in the face of this, it is crucial that we look into this question: is it only sentimentality that makes those who love and cherish books believe they are superior to any other form of communication in almost all circum-stances? Given the two advances in communications of recent times—the computer and the Internet—and anticipating how these will be enhanced and extended in the near (very near) future, with nearly any piece of text available anywhere at any time, in a form portable, light, and ubiquitous, how will books measure up? If they really are superior, then we can anticipate a future in which books will endure. If not, then the new generation will compare the various forms and make their choices, and they may well select other forms that are in some ways more convenient. Some defenders of books speak of how utilitarian books are as deliverers of information ("look how easy it is to turn a page") or how durable a book is. There is something both charming and disappointing in these defenses: all they point to is the next ergonomic frontier, the next "big new thing" to come out of the lab.

Thus, if this collection is to be also a celebration of books, and not an extended epitaph, we are going to have to offer some reason for believing that books will endure and survive the current spate of technological wonder-working on their own merits. We will argue that books are better than these other systems and that reading a book is so unique and special an experience that readers will keep reading books and looking to books for the kind of insight and experience that only books can offer. It seems presumptuous for anyone to have to remind some of the more venerable editors what is so wonderful, so uniquely wonderful, about books, but here is what we have to say.

A book is more than just a bound collection of

paper pages and printed information. Reading a book is like getting to know a person over time, every moment of which is informed by many things beyond what is at that moment being said: manner, body language, dress, handshake, smile, eye contact, the entire visage; as well as the whole history of the relationship up to that moment and its expectations for the future. One of the steps in the development of a mature and balanced personality is learning to look beyond the strictly superficial aspects of a person, to appreciate his or her wisdom, character, abilities, and other more important qualities. But it's all there before us, and we'd be less than honest with ourselves if we did not acknowledge that we're influenced by everything. (The trick is to do the right thing and act righteously anyway.)

The same is true in encounters with books. The entire book is before us, and we are influenced by the total package: the jacket; the cover; the endpapers (decorative or not); the quality, color, cut, and texture of the paper; the size of the page; the size, font, and spacing of text and the layout of each page; the way the chapters open and the way notes and bibliographic materials are organized; whether and how illustrations are presented, and how they are captioned. Anyone who thinks these elements don't really matter will have no objection to their only child's wedding being a come-as-you-are affair at a local diner. We take the book design for granted until a poor design destroys a book. Similarly, we take our sensual experience of books for granted until electronic publishing destroys that experience. The availability of desktop publishing programs allows anyone with a PC to delude himself into thinking he is capable of designing a book, and the unfortunate results of this kind of amateurism are books with wildly inappropriate type styles and a fast-food approach to make-up.

Holding a book in your hand puts you in contact with a train of thought and a narrative thread, and a sensitive reader is in contact with the full length of that thread at any given moment, on any given page in the course of reading a book. (Who hasn't felt the remaining pages between thumb and fingers and cursed that there was so little—or so much—left?) Reading a book will often require rereading earlier passages, ones that are particularly important or involved. A practiced reader will note the organization of a book at the outset and monitor his or her relative position at every point in the reading. Does this matter? Well, many people are familiar with portions of the ceiling of the Sistine Chapel, perhaps even all of it, through photographs, but seeing it in real life is a completely unique experience. In fact, it is only when we see it as the artist intended it to be seen that we are truly able to appreciate its magnificence, and to recognize the extent to which the whole is greater than the sum of its parts.

Similarly, when reading we combine otherwise meaningless letters into words that have meaning, words into sentences that express ideas, and sentences into paragraphs conveying themes. Paragraphs, in turn, are combined into chapters, which themselves are joined together into what we call a book—something truly magnificent to behold. Thus, like the Sistine Chapel, a book—any book, and every book—is more than the sum of its parts. And it is the presence of the author in the "person" of the book that makes this so.

The book's thesis, theme, or story has an irreducible wholeness and an identity that depends on being read more or less as the author intended. The books on our shelves represent in more than a symbolic or metaphorical sense the authors who wrote them—not their physical appearance or their foibles and habits (though sometimes that may be captured in a book as well), but the totality of the message contained between their covers. Tactile access to the entire book puts us literally in *touch* with the stream of argument and the flow of thought as they run through its pages. In this view, and to our way of thinking, libraries are not quiet places at all. Their shelves fairly clamor with the voices of many authors, calling out their ideas, themes, stories, morals, and lessons.

There is a rabbinic legend, a midrash, that has it that at Sinai, when the Israelites received the Ten Commandments directly from God, they did not experience them as a string of syllables, words, and sentences. Miraculously, they received the thought whole and undifferentiated. Something very much like this happens in the relationship between the reader and the book. When the unseen author's control of the content meets the reader's control of the place, time, pace, direction, and volume at which he reads, it's a revelation, a miracle indeed. So we afford the book a special place of honor, even—or especially—in this electronic age.

For *A Passion for Books* we asked Ray Bradbury to contribute a foreword because he was the author of *Fahrenheit 451*, a novel in which books are outlawed, hunted, and burned. In the finale, readers meet a group of people—"living books" they're called—each of whom has committed a book to memory for the purpose of reciting it to others to keep it alive. This stark illustration of such a pure and total commitment to books gave us the idea of compiling a list of those books that our friends and associates would be prepared to commit to memory. We were somewhat surprised, in the process of doing so, to learn that this was not the same as asking people what their favorite books were, or which books they thought the most important to preserve, or even which books they thought were the best. We realized, in fact, that asking someone for which book they would want to become a "living book" is really asking them which book is most alive and like a living presence to them. The imagery that Bradbury uses so effectively, paradoxically enough, mirrors the reality of what happens when we read a book. It was this quality that Heine may have had in mind when he warned that "wherever they burn books, they will also, in the end, burn human beings."

What of all this survives into the electronic realm? Very, very little. Certainly the hum and distance of the computer screen removes the humanity from the reading experience. The perfect electronic delivery system—humless, glareless, sharp, easy—may deliver words and the ideas may be there on the screen, but this larger unit of communication, the one that conveys the totality of the book and provides the human dimension, is lost.

It's not good enough simply to convey information. Living information, ideas born of flesh-and-blood thinkers, are best embodied and effectively communicated in physical form. Books have this capability; electronics do not. There are many ways in which electronics can enhance a reading experience and, lord knows, computers and the Internet have aided modern research immeasurably. But books bring authors and readers together in a wholly unique way. It is this encounter that is one of the most exhilarating and endlessly fascinating qualities of literature.

Long live books!

—THE EDITORS
Cortlandt Manor, New York
Riverdale, New York
August 2000

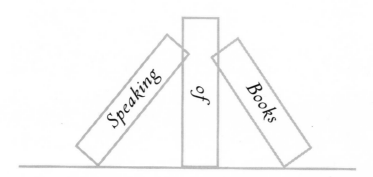

When a man's fortunes fail, let him first sell his gold and jewels, then let him sell his land and his estate, and then his clothes and his belongings. When he has nothing left, only then let him sell his books.

RABBI JUDAH THE PIOUS, *Sefer Hasidim*

1

In Praise of Books

ALL THE GLORY OF THE WORLD would be buried in
oblivion," wrote Richard de Bury in *Philobiblon*, "unless
God had provided mortals with the remedy of books."
Although it was completed in 1345, a hundred years *before*
Gutenberg printed his first Bible, de Bury's classic paean
to books was not published until 1473, by which time
books were being printed all over Europe, unleashing a
revolution that would shake the world.

And in every generation since de Bury's new voices
have joined the chorus, new readers—and writers—
expressing the pleasures they take in books. In the
seventeenth century, for example, John Milton referred
to books as "the precious life-blood of a master spirit,"
while in the eighteenth Joseph Addison called them

"the legacies that a great genius leaves to mankind."
In the nineteenth century, Gladstone considered them
"delightful society," and Richard le Gallienne "immortal
nightingales that sing for ever to the rose of life."

Even today, more than 650 years after de Bury first
put pen to paper, and despite the advent of technology
that some claim will replace books, there are still those—
and will continue to be those—who believe, as Thomas
Carlyle did, that "of the things which man can do or
make here below, by far the most momentous, wonderful,
and worthy are the things called books."

Books are the legacies that a great genius leaves to
mankind, which are delivered down from generation to
generation, as presents to the posterity of those who are
yet unborn.

JOSEPH ADDISON, in *The Spectator*, September 10, 1711

[The book is] at the head of all the pleasures which
offer themselves to the man of liberal education; in
variety, durability, and facility of attainment, no other
can stand in competition with it; and even in intensity
it is inferior to few.

JOHN AIKEN, *Letters from a Father to a Son* (1796)

Monuments of wit and learning are more durable than the monuments of power or of the hands. Have not the verses of Homer continued twenty-five hundred years, or more, without the loss of a syllable or letter; during which time infinite palaces, temples, castles, cities, have been decayed and demolished? It is not possible to have the true pictures of Cyrus, Alexander, Caesar, no, nor of the kings or great personages of much later years; for the originals cannot last, and the copies cannot but leese of the life and truth. But the images of men's wits and knowledge remain in books, exempted from the wrong of time and capable of perpetual renovation.

FRANCIS BACON, "Of the Advancement of Learning," *Essays* (1625)

A book is good company. It is full of conversation without loquacity. It comes to your longing with full instruction, but pursues you never.

HENRY WARD BEECHER, *Proverbs from Plymouth Pulpit* (1887)

Books are the windows through which the soul looks out. A home without books is like a room without windows.

HENRY WARD BEECHER, *The Sermons of Henry Ward Beecher,* (1870) [See Cicero, p. 7]

[Books] are men of higher stature,
And the only men that speak aloud for future times
    to hear.

ELIZABETH BARRETT BROWNING, *Lady Geraldine's Courtship* (1870)

A good book is the purest essence of a human soul.

THOMAS CARLYLE, in a speech in support of the London Library, June 24, 1840, in *Carlyle and the London Library*, by F. Harrison (1907)

All that Mankind has done, thought, gained, or been is lying as in magic preservation in the pages of Books.

THOMAS CARLYLE, "The Hero as a Man of Letters," *On Heroes, Hero-Worship, and the Heroic* (1841)

Are we not driven to the conclusion that of the things which man can do or make here below, by far the most momentous, wonderful, and worthy are the things called Books?

THOMAS CARLYLE, "The Hero as a Man of Letters," *On Heroes, Hero-Worship, and the Heroic* (1841)

In books lies the *soul* of the whole Past Time; the articulate audible voice of the Past, when the body and material substance of it has altogether vanished like a dream.

THOMAS CARLYLE, "The Hero as a Man of Letters," *On Heroes, Hero-Worship, and the Heroic* (1841)

Let every man, if possible, gather some good books under his roof, and obtain access for himself and family to some social library. Almost any luxury should be sacrificed to this.

WILLIAM ELLERY CHANNING, *Self-Culture* (1838)

A room without books is like a body without a soul.

CICERO [See Henry Ward Beecher, p. 5]

Of all the inanimate objects, of all men's creations, books are the nearest to us, for they contain our very thoughts, our ambitions, our indignations, our illusions, our fidelity to truth, and our persistent leaning towards error. But most of all they resemble us in their precarious hold on life.

JOSEPH CONRAD, *Notes on Life and Letters* (1921)

A library of wisdom is more precious than all wealth, and all things that are desirable cannot be compared to it. Whoever therefore claims to be zealous of truth, of happiness, of wisdom or knowledge, aye even of the faith, must needs become a lover of books.

RICHARD DE BURY, *Philobiblon* (1473)

All the glory of the world would be buried in oblivion, unless God had provided mortals with the remedy of books.

RICHARD DE BURY, *Philobiblon* (1473)

Books do actually consume air and exhale perfumes.

EUGENE FIELD, *Love Affairs of a Bibliomaniac* (1896)

Books are delightful society. If you go into a room and find it full of books—even without taking them from the shelves they seem to speak to you, to bid you welcome. They seem to tell you that they have got something inside their covers that will be good for you, and that they are willing and desirous to impart to you. Value them much.

WILLIAM GLADSTONE

$\mathbf{A}$ book is a lovely thing—a garden stocked with beautiful flowers, a magic carpet on which to fly away to unknown climes.

FRANK GRUBER, *The Mask of Dimitrios* (screenplay) (1944)

$\mathbf{A}$mong the many worlds which man did not receive as a gift of nature, but which he created out of his own mind, the world of books is the greatest. . . . Without the word, without the writing of books, there is no history, there is no concept of humanity. And if anyone wants to try to enclose in a small space in a single house or single room, the history of the human spirit and to make it his own, he can only do this in the form of a collection of books.

HERMANN HESSE, "The Magic of the Book," *My Belief: Essays on Life and Art* (1974)

$\mathbf{B}$ooks are never out of humour; never envious or jealous, they answer all questions with readiness; they reveal the secrets of Nature, the events of the past; they teach us how to live and how to die; they dispel melancholy by their mirth, and amuse by their wit; they prepare the soul to suffer everything and desire nothing; they introduce us to ourselves; they uphold the downcast, and restrain the conceited by warning that days are swift and life short; and all they ask in return is a quiet corner where they may be safe from the attacks of their enemies.

HOLBROOK JACKSON, *The Anatomy of Bibliomania* (1930)
[See Francesco Petrarch, pp. 12–13, and Laurence Sterne, p. 14]

Without them, not only the solitary, but the social grow needy of mind and impoverished of spirit, for books are the granaries in which the harvest of mankind is stored; they are the best, readiest, surest way to choose inward riches which all wise men approve.

HOLBROOK JACKSON, *The Anatomy of Bibliomania* (1930)

The love of books is a love which requires neither justification, apology, nor defence. It is a good thing in itself; a possession to be thankful for, to rejoice over, to be proud of, and to sing praises for. With this love in his heart no man is ever poor, ever without friends, or the means of making his life lovely, beautiful, and happy.

JOHN ALFRED LANGFORD

Books . . . those miraculous memories of high thoughts and golden moods; those magical shells, tremulous with the secrets of the ocean of life; those love-letters that pass from hand to hand of a thousand lovers that never meet; those honeycombs of dreams; those orchards of knowledge; those still-beating hearts of the noble dead; those mysterious signals that beckon along the darksome pathways of the past; voices through which the myriad lispings of the earth find perfect speech; oracles through which its mysteries call like voices in moonlit woods; prisms of beauty; urns stored with all the sweets of all the summers of time; immortal nightingales that sing for ever to the rose of life.

RICHARD LE GALLIENNE, *Prose Fancies* (1894)

For books are more than books, they are the life
The very heart and core of ages past,
The reason why men lived and worked and died,
The essence and quintessence of their lives.

AMY LOWELL, "The Boston Athenaeum," *A Dome of Many-Coloured Glass* (1912)

As good almost kill a man as kill a good book. Who kills a man kills a reasonable creature, God's image; but he who destroys a good book, kills reason itself, kills the image of God, as it were in the eye.

JOHN MILTON, *Areopagitica* (1644)

Books are not absolutely dead things, but do contain a potency of life in them to be as active as that soul was whose progeny they are; nay, they do preserve as in a vial the purest efficacy and extraction of that living intellect that bred them.

JOHN MILTON, *Areopagitica* (1644)

Many a man lives a burden to the earth; but a good book is the precious life-blood of a master spirit, embalmed and treasured up on purpose to a life beyond life.

JOHN MILTON, *Areopagitica* (1644)

It is . . . a pure and unmixed pleasure to have a goodly volume lying before you, and to know that you may open it if you please, and need not open it unless you please. It is a resource against ennui, if ennui should come upon you. To have the resource and not to feel the ennui, to enjoy your bottle in the present, and your book in the indefinite future, is a delightful condition of human existence.

THOMAS LOVE PEACOCK, *Crotchet Castle* (1831)

I have friends, whose society is extremely agreeable to me: they are of all ages, and of every country. They have distinguished themselves both in the cabinet and in the field, and obtained high honors for their knowledge of the sciences. It is easy to gain access to them; for they are always at my service, and I admit them to my company, and dismiss them from it, whenever I please. They are never troublesome, but immediately answer every question I ask them. Some relate to me the events of past ages, while others reveal to me the secrets of nature. Some, by their vivacity, drive away my cares and exhilarate my spirits, while others give fortitude to my mind, and teach me the important lesson how to restrain my desires, and to depend wholly on myself. They open to me, in short, the various avenues of all the arts and sciences, and upon their information I safely rely, in all emergencies. In return for all these services, they only ask me to accommodate them with a convenient chamber in some corner of my humble habitation, where they may repose in peace: for these friends are more delighted by the tranquility of retirement, than by the tumults of society.

FRANCESCO PETRARCH, in *The Life of Petrarch* by Susanna Dobson (1775) [See Holbrook Jackson, pp. 9–10, and Laurence Sterne, p. 14]

Bread and books: food for the body and food for the soul—what could be more worthy of our respect, and even love?

SALMAN RUSHDIE, *Imaginary Homelands* (1992)

While you converse with lords and dukes,
I have their betters here—my books.

THOMAS SHERIDAN

I often derive a peculiar satisfaction in conversing with
the ancient and modern dead, who yet live and speak
excellently in their works. My neighbours think me *often
alone,* and yet at such times I am in company with more
than five hundred mutes—each of whom, at my pleasure,
communicates his ideas to me by dumb signs.... I lay
hands on fifty of them sometimes in an evening, and
handle them as I like; they never complain of ill-usage,
and when dismissed from my presence—though ever
so abruptly—take no offence. Such convenience is not
to be enjoyed—nor such liberty to be taken—with
the living.

LAURENCE STERNE, *Letters of the Late Rev. Laurence
Sterne,* edited by Lydia Sterne Medalle (1775) [See Holbrook
Jackson, pp. 9–10, and Francesco Petrarch, pp. 12–13]

I prefer books to people because a book doesn't
double-cross you.

DONALD OGDEN STEWART, *Without Love* (screenplay)
(1945)

An honest book's the noblest work of Man.

HENRY DAVID THOREAU, in a letter to his sister Helen,
January 23, 1840

A good book is the best of friends, the same today
and forever.

MARTIN FARQUHAR TUPPER, "Of Reading,"
Proverbial Philosophy (1832–1842)

It is with the reading of books the same as with looking
at pictures; one must, without doubt, without hesitations,
with assurance, admire what is beautiful.

VINCENT VAN GOGH

In Praise of Books

2

The Pleasures of Buying and Owning Books

THERE ARE SOME INDIVIDUALS—or so we have heard—who can enjoy reading a borrowed book as much as they do one of their own. To be honest, we find this rather difficult to believe, as do many other bibliophiles (not to say bibliomanes). In fact, there are many who believe that the pleasures of owning and buying books can be even greater than those of reading them.

Note that we say *can*, for we do so for a reason. Although there are many of us who occasionally—even frequently—buy books simply to have them rather than to read them, we believe that at the heart of the true bibliophile's devotion to books is the love of reading, and that, as Robertson Davies says, "the only collector who really matters" is the one "who loves books, and reads them."

Nevertheless, while we recognize that there are certainly pleasures to be had in reading any book, even one that belongs to someone else, that pleasure is nothing compared to the pleasure of reading one's *own* book, as many here attest.

———

I am a philistine in taste, I suppose, for I never can bring myself nowadays to buy a second-hand book. For dusty old tomes, I go to the public library; but my own private books must be sweet and clean. There are many who prefer old copies, who revel in the inscribed names of former owners, and prize their marginal annotations. If there be some special sentimental associations connected with these factors, if the books be heirlooms, and the annotations come from a vanished, but beloved, hand, then the old book becomes an old love. But in most cases these things seem to me the defects of youth, not the virtues of age; for they are usually too recent to be venerable, though they are just old enough to disfigure. Let my books be young, fresh, and fragrant in their virgin purity, unspotted by the world. If my copy is to be soiled, I want to do all the soiling myself.

ISRAEL ABRAHAMS, *The Book of Delight and Other Papers* (1912)

Own all the books you can, use all the books you own, and as many more as you can get.

ANONYMOUS

Buying books, before you can pay for them, promotes caution. You do not feel quite at liberty to take them home. You are married. Your wife keeps an account-book. She knows to a penny what you can and what you can not afford. She has no "speculation" in your eyes. Plain figures make desperate work with airy "Somehows." It is a matter of no small skill and experience to get your books home, and into their proper places undiscovered. Perhaps the blundering Express brings them to the door just at evening. "What is it, my dear?" she says to you. "Oh! Nothing—a few books that I can not do without." That smile! A true housewife, that loves her husband, can smile a whole arithmetic at him in one look! Of course she insists, in the kindest way, in sympathizing with you in your literary acquisitions. She cuts the strings of the bundle and of your heart, and out comes the whole story. You have bought a complete set of costly English books, full bound in calf, extra gilt. You are caught, and feel very much as if bound in calf yourself, and admirably lettered.

HENRY WARD BEECHER, *Star Papers; or, Experiences of Art and Nature* (1855)

I love my books as drinkers love their wine;
The more I drink, the more they seem divine;
With joy elate my soul in love runs o'er,
And each fresh draught is sweeter than before.

FRANCIS BENNOCH, "My Books," *The Storm and
Other Poems*

An ordinary man can . . . surround himself with two
thousand books . . . and thenceforward have at least one
place in the world in which it is possible to be happy.

AUGUSTINE BIRRELL

Good as it is to inherit a library, it is better to
collect one.

AUGUSTINE BIRRELL, "Book-Buying," *Obiter
Dicta* (1887)

The possession of a book becomes a substitute for
reading it.

ANTHONY BURGESS, "The Book Is Not for Reading,"
The New York Times Book Review, December 4, 1966

[To produce the true] elements of enjoyment, the
book-hunter's treasures must not be his mere property,

they must be his achievements—each one of them recalling the excitement of the chase and the happiness of success.

JOHN HILL BURTON, *The Book-Hunter* (1862)

What shall I do with all my books?" was the question; and the answer, "Read them," sobered the questioner. But if you cannot read them, at any rate handle them and, as it were, fondle them. Peer into them. Let them fall open where they will. Read on from the first sentence that arrests the eye. Then turn to another. Make a voyage of discovery, taking soundings of uncharted seas. Set them back on their shelves with your own hands. Arrange them on your own plan, so that if you do not know what is in them, you at least know where they are. If they cannot be your friends, let them at any rate be your acquaintances. If they cannot enter the circle of your life, do not deny them at least a nod of recognition.

WINSTON S. CHURCHILL, "Hobbies," *Thoughts and Adventures* (1932)

Keep your books and do not despair of my making them mine some day; if I ever do, I shall be the richest of millionaires, and shan't envy any man his manors and meadows.

CICERO, *Letters to Atticus*

Ah yet, ere I descend to the grave
May I a small house and large garden have;
And a few friends, and many books, both true,
Both wise, and both delightful too!

ABRAHAM COWLEY, *The Wish* (1647)

One book at a time, or a very few at a time—there's
the ideal way! Bargain a bit, grouse a bit; go home and
consult the oracles of bibliography and the auction
records; then go back with the gleam of the hunter in
your eye and bring down your bird. There is no other
method. You must have the urge to rummage about.
You must learn to love the feel of old books; the smell of
them must be unto you a delicious aroma. But at first
confine your prowling—if you can—to times when your
pocketbook is lean. Your resistance is apt to be very low
when the exchequer overflows. You will find it much
easier to stick to a one-book or one-author plan if you
buy only when you are comparatively hard up.

BARTON W. CURRIE, *Fishers of Books* (1931)

No dearness of price ought to hinder a man from the
buying of books, if he has the money that is demanded
for them, unless it be to withstand the malice of the seller
or to await a more favourable opportunity of buying.

RICHARD DE BURY, *Philobiblon* (1473)

Sweeter than thy unguents and cosmetics and Sabean perfumes is the smell of those old books of mine.

EUGENE FIELD, *Love Affairs of a Bibliomaniac* (1896)

When of a morning I awaken I cast my eyes about my room to see how fare my beloved treasures, and as I cry cheerily to them, "Good-day to you, sweet friends!" how lovingly they beam upon me.

EUGENE FIELD, *Love Affairs of a Bibliomaniac* (1896)

Books are not entirely valued or intimately loved unless they are ranged about us as we sit at home.

SIR EDMUND GOSSE, *The Library of Edmund Gosse* (1924)

I must have my literary harem . . . where my favorites await my moments of leisure and pleasure—my scarce and precious editions, my luxurious typographical masterpieces; my Delilahs, that take my head in their lap; the pleasant story-tellers and the like; the books I love because they are fair to look upon, prized by collectors, endeared by old associations, secret treasures that nobody else knows anything about; books, in short, that I like for insufficient reasons it may be, but peremptorily, and mean to like and to love and to cherish till death do us part.

OLIVER WENDELL HOLMES, SR., *The Poet at the Breakfast-Table* (1872)

What a happy thing ought it not to be to have exclusive possession of a book. . . . Think of the pleasure of not only being with it in general, of having by far the greater part of its company, but of having it entirely to oneself; of always saying internally, "It is my property."

LEIGH HUNT, *Wedded to Books* (c. 1850)

It is pleasanter to eat one's peas out of one's own garden, than to buy them by the peck at Covent Garden; and a book reads the better, which is our own, and has been so long known to us, that we know the topography of its blots and dogs' ears, and can trace the dirt in it to having read it at tea with buttered muffins, or over a pipe.

CHARLES LAMB, in a letter to Samuel Taylor Coleridge, *The Letters of Charles Lamb*, edited by E. V. Lucas (1935)

I enjoy [books], as a miser doth his gold; to know, that I may enjoy them when I list; my mind is settled and satisfied by the right of possession.

MICHEL EYQUEM DE MONTAIGNE, "Of Three Commerces or Societies," *Essays* (1580)

The one best and sufficient reason for a man to buy a book is because he thinks he will be happier with it than without it.

A. EDWARD NEWTON, *The Amenities of Book-Collecting and Kindred Affections* (1918)

To gain glory by books you must not only possess them but know them; their lodgings must be in your brain and not on your book-shelf.

FRANCESCO PETRARCH, IN *The Great Book-Collectors* by Charles and Mary Elton (1893)

Wear the old coat and buy the new book.

AUSTIN PHELPS, *The Theory of Preaching; Lectures on Homiletics* (1881)

There is no time so good to read a book as when you have just bought it and brought it home.

SIR WALTER RALEIGH, *Letters of Sir Walter Raleigh*, edited by Lady Raleigh (1926)

The very cheapness of literature is making even wise people forget that if a book is worth reading, it is worth buying. No book is worth anything which is not worth *much;* nor is it serviceable, until it has been read, and re-read, and loved, and loved again; and marked, so that you can refer to the passages you want in it.

JOHN RUSKIN, *Sesame and Lilies* (1865)

We ought not to get books too cheaply. No book, I believe, is ever worth half so much to its reader as one that has been coveted for a year at a bookstall, and bought out of saved halfpence; and perhaps a day or two's fasting. That's the way to get at the cream of a book.

JOHN RUSKIN, *A Joy for Ever and Its Price on the Market* (1857)

Talk of the happiness of getting a great prize in the lottery! What is that to opening a box of books! The joy upon lifting up the cover must be something like what we shall feel when Peter the Porter opens the door upstairs, and says, Please to walk in, sir.

ROBERT SOUTHEY, in a letter to Samuel Taylor Coleridge

These books of mine ... are not drawn up here for display, however much the pride of the eye may be gratified in beholding them; they are on actual service. Whenever they may be dispersed, there is not one among them that will ever be more comfortably lodged, or more highly prized by its possessor.

ROBERT SOUTHEY, *Sir Thomas More: or, Colloquies on the Progress and Prospects of Society* (1829)

[Is] there any excitement to compare with the opening of a fresh parcel of books?

WILLIAM TARG

The true bibliophile loves the existence of a book more than its form and content; under no circumstances must he read it (is not something similar true of every great love?).

FRANZ WERFEL

The Pleasures of Buying and Owning Books

3

What to Read

TO TRUE BIBLIOPHILES, the seemingly simple act
of selecting a book to read can present a considerable
problem. Because they usually own more books than
they will ever have the time to read, and thus have a
plethora of titles to choose from, being faced with
making a decision to pluck one book from the shelf
rather than another can throw a book lover into a
serious quandary.

Recommending books, on the other hand, is rarely
a problem, and most bibliophiles are always more than
ready to suggest favorite books to their friends. And
those recommendations—be they fiction, history, science,
poetry, or whatever—are invariably as different as those
who recommend them. They are so different, in fact,

that it might be well for us to remember Virginia Woolf's counsel that "the only advice, indeed, that one person can give another about reading is to take no advice. . . . After all, what laws can be laid down about books?"

Whatever wisdom may be contained in those sentiments, if Woolf's advice has been followed at all, it is to a much greater extent in theory than in practice. For there are a great many people who believe they know best what everyone *else* should read—if not specific titles, then at least types of books—and some of their suggestions are contained in the pages that follow.

Alonso of Aragon was wont to say, in commendation of Age, that Age appeared to be best in four things; Old wood best to burn, old wine to drink, old friends to trust, and old authors to read.

FRANCIS BACON, *Apothegms* (1624)

Make careful choice of the books which you read. Let the Holy Scriptures ever have the pre-eminence, and next them, the solid, lively, heavenly treatises which best expound and apply the Scriptures: and next those, the credible histories, especially of the Church, and tractates upon inferior sciences and arts: but take heed of the poison of false teachers, which would corrupt your understanding: and of vain romances, play-books, and false stories, which may bewitch your fantasies and corrupt your hearts.

RICHARD BAXTER, *Christian Directory* (1846)

Of all odd crazes, the craze to be for ever reading new books is one of the oddest.

AUGUSTINE BIRRELL, "Books Old and New," *The Collected Essays and Addresses* (1922) [See Frederic Harrison, p. 36]

In science, read by preference the newest works; in literature, the oldest. The classic literature is always modern. New books revive and re-decorate old ideas; old books suggest and invigorate new ideas.

EDWARD BULWER-LYTTON, "Hints on Mental Culture," *Caxtoniana* (1863)

The best books for man are not always those which the wise recommend, but often those which meet the peculiar wants, the natural thirsts of his mind, and therefore awaken interest and rival thought.

WILLIAM ELLERY CHANNING

[Avoid] those trivial futile books, published by idle or necessitous authors, for the amusement of idle or ignorant readers; such sorts of book swarm and buzz about one every day; flap them away; they have no sting.

PHILIP DORMER STANHOPE, EARL OF CHESTERFIELD, *Letters to His Son* (1774)

Buy good books, and read them; the best books are the commonest, and the last editions are always the best, if the editors are not blockheads, for they may profit from the former. But take care not to understand editions and title-pages too well. It always smells of pedantry, and never of learning.

PHILIP DORMER STANHOPE, EARL OF CHESTERFIELD, *Letters to His Son* (1774)

The easiest books are generally the best, for whatever author is obscure and difficult in his own language certainly does not think clearly.

PHILIP DORMER STANHOPE, EARL OF CHESTERFIELD, *Letters to His Son* (1774)

Looking back on a world and wasted life, I realize that I have especially sinned in neglecting to read novels.

G. K. CHESTERTON, "On Philosophy Versus Fiction," *All Is Grist* (1932)

It is a good thing for an uneducated man to read books of quotations. . . . The quotations when engraved upon the memory give you good thoughts. They also make you anxious to read the authors and look for more.

WINSTON S. CHURCHILL, *Roving Commission: My Early Life* (1930)

[A]n excellent book (and the remark holds almost equally good of a Raphael as of a Milton) is like a well-chosen and well-tended fruit tree. Its fruits are not of one season only. With the due and natural intervals, we may recur to it year after year, and it will supply the same nourishment and the same gratification, if only we ourselves return to it with the same healthful appetite.

SAMUEL TAYLOR COLERIDGE

We should choose our books as we would our companions, for their sterling and intrinsic merit.

CHARLES CALEB COLTON, *Lacon: or, Many Things in Few Words; Addressed to Those Who Think* (1823)

Read no history: nothing but biography, for that is life without theory.

BENJAMIN DISRAELI, *Contarini Fleming* (1844)

Be sure, then, to read no mean books. Shun the spawn of the press on the gossip of the hour. Do not read what you shall learn, without asking, in the street and the train.

RALPH WALDO EMERSON, "Books," *Society and Solitude* (1870)

The three practical rules, then, which I have to offer, are—(1) Never read any book that is not a year old. (2) Never read any but famed books. (3) Never read any but what you like; or, in Shakespeare's phrase,

> "No profit where is no pleasure ta'en:
> In brief, sir, study what you most affect."

RALPH WALDO EMERSON, "Books," *Society and Solitude* (1870)

The vital thing is that you have your own favorites— books that are real and genuine, each one brimful of the inspiration of a great soul. Keep these books on a shelf convenient for use, and read them again and again until you have saturated your mind with their wisdom and beauty. So may you come into the true Kingdom of Culture, whose gates never swing open to the pedant or the bigot. So may you be armed against the worst blows that fate can deal you in this world.

GEORGE HAMLIN FITCH, *Comfort Found in Good Old Books* (1911)

What did passengers do on long voyages when there were no novels? They must bless the man that invented them.

J. A. FROUDE, *Oceana* (1886) [See Dr. Samuel Johnson, p. 39]

The volumes of antiquity, like medals, may very well amuse the curious, but the works of the moderns, like the current coin of a kingdom, are much better for immediate use.

OLIVER GOLDSMITH, *The Citizen of the World* (1762)

I have ever gained the most profit and the most pleasure also, from the books which have made me think the most; and, when the difficulties have once been overcome, these are the books which have struck the deepest root, not only in my memory but likewise in my affections.

A. W. AND J. C. HARE, *Guesses at Truth* (1827)

A man can hardly be said to know the 12th Mass or the 9th Symphony, by virtue of having once heard them played ten years ago; he can hardly be said to take air and exercise because he took a country walk once last Autumn. And so he can hardly be said to know Scott or Shakespeare, Molière or Cervantes, when he once read them since the close of his schooldays, or amidst the daily grind of his professional life. The immortal and universal poets of our race are to be read and re-read till their music and their spirit are a part of our nature; they are to be thought over and digested till we live in the world they created for us.

FREDERIC HARRISON, *The Choice of Books and Other Literary Pieces* (1886)

Idle reading debilitates and corrupts the mind for all wholesome reading.

FREDERIC HARRISON, *The Choice of Books and Other Literary Pieces* (1886)

This literary prurience after new print unmans us for the enjoyment of the old songs chanted forth in the sunrise of human imagination.

FREDERIC HARRISON, *The Choice of Books and Other Literary Pieces* (1886) [See Augustine Birrell, p. 31]

All that wearies profoundly is to be condemned for reading. The mind profits little by what is termed heavy reading.

LAFCADIO HEARN, "Reading," in the *New Orleans Item*, April 22, 1881

The first thing which a scholar should bear in mind is that a book ought not to be read for mere amusement. Half-educated persons read for amusement, and are not to be blamed for it; they are incapable of appreciating the deeper qualities that belong to a really great literature. But a young man who has passed through a course of university training should discipline himself at an early day never to read for mere amusement. And once the habit of the discipline has been formed, he will even find it impossible to read for mere amusement. He will then impatiently throw down any book from which he cannot obtain intellectual food, any book which does not make an appeal to the higher emotions and to his intellect. But on the other hand, the habit of reading for amusement becomes with thousands of people exactly the same kind of habit as wine-drinking or opium-smoking; it is like a narcotic, something that helps to pass the time, something that keeps up a perpetual condition of dreaming, something that eventually results in destroying all capacity for thought, giving exercise only to the surface parts of the mind, and leaving the deeper springs of feeling and the higher faculties of perception unemployed.

LAFCADIO HEARN, *Talks to Writers* (1920)

I am not my brother's keeper; and if there were still less readers than there are, and books still less accessible, I should be content, for every true reader will work out his own salvation with taste and affection his best guides.

HOLBROOK JACKSON, *The Anatomy of Bibliomania* (1930)

Read what you like, because you like it, seeking no other reason and no other profit than the experience of reading. If you enjoy the experience it is well; but whether you enjoy it or not the experience is worth having. But I do not rule out reading with a more definite purpose, such as study or research. That which suits your purpose is best, for happiness, pleasure, joy, prefer to come unawares; they are shy of pursuit and resentful in captivity. And what is enjoined for reading is good also for collecting. Collect what you like, seeking neither profit nor applause. That is all.

HOLBROOK JACKSON, *The Anatomy of Bibliomania* (1930)

Books that you may carry to the fire, and hold readily in your hand, are the most useful after all.

DR. SAMUEL JOHNSON, in *The Life of Samuel Johnson* by James Boswell (1791)

If you are to have but one book with you upon a journey, let it be a book of science, for when you have read through a book of entertainment, you know it, and it can do no more for you; but a book of science is inexhaustible.

DR. SAMUEL JOHNSON, in *The Life of Samuel Johnson* by James Boswell (1791) [See J. A. Froude, p. 35]

A man ought to read just as inclination leads him; for what he reads as a task will do him little good.

DR. SAMUEL JOHNSON, in *The Life of Samuel Johnson* by James Boswell (1791)

Every work of genius, be it epic or didactic, is too long if it cannot be read in one day.

LAURENT JOUBERT, *Selected Thoughts* (c. 1580)

What to Read

[W]e ought to read only the kind of books that wound and stab us. . . . We need the books that affect us like a disaster, that grieve us deeply, like the death of someone we loved more than ourselves, like being banished into forests far from everyone, like a suicide. A book must be the axe for the frozen sea inside us.

FRANZ KAFKA, in a letter to Oskar Pollak, January 27, 1904

A wise man will select his books, for he would not wish to class them all under the sacred name of friends. Some can be accepted only as acquaintances. The best books of all kinds are taken to the heart, and cherished as his most precious possessions. Others to be chatted with for a time, to spend a few pleasant hours with, and laid aside, but not forgotten.

JOHN ALFRED LANGFORD

Never judge a cover by its book.

FRAN LEBOWITZ, *Metropolitan Life* (1978)

I would sooner read a time-table or a catalogue than nothing at all. . . . They are much more entertaining than half the novels that are written.

W. SOMERSET MAUGHAM, *The Summing Up* (1938)

I love no books but such as are pleasant and easie, and which tickle me, or such as comfort and counsell me, to direct my life and death.

MICHEL EYQUEM DE MONTAIGNE

As sheer casual reading matter, I still find the English dictionary the most interesting book in our language.

ALBERT JAY NOCK, *Memoirs of a Superfluous Man* (1943)

Huge volumes, like the ox roasted whole at Bartholomew Fair, may proclaim plenty of labour, but afford less of what is delicate, savoury, and well-concocted, than smaller pieces.

FRANCIS OSBORNE, *Advice to a Son*

It becomes you to be wise, to smell, feel and have in estimation, these fair, godly books, stuffed with high conceptions.

FRANÇOIS RABELAIS

Choose an author as you choose a friend.

WENTWORTH DILLON, EARL OF ROSCOMMON, "Essay on Translated Verse" (1684)

What to Read

For all books are divisible into two classes, the books of the hour, and the books of all time. Mark this distinction—it is not one of quality only. It is not merely the bad book that does not last, and the good one that does. . . . There are good books for the hour, and good ones for all time; bad books for the hour, and bad ones for all time.

JOHN RUSKIN, *Sesame and Lilies* (1865)

Life being very short, and the quiet hours of it few, we ought to waste none of them in reading valueless books.

JOHN RUSKIN

You should only read what is truly good or what is frankly bad.

GERTRUDE STEIN, in *A Moveable Feast* by Ernest Hemingway (1964)

Read the best books first, or you may not have a chance to read them at all.

HENRY DAVID THOREAU, *A Week on the Concord and Merrimack Rivers* (1849)

The only advice, indeed, that one person can give another about reading is to take no advice. . . . After all, what laws can be laid down about books?

VIRGINIA WOOLF, *The Second Common Reader* (1932)

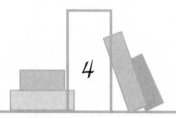

The Influence of Books

"HOW MANY A MAN," says Thoreau in *Walden*, "has dated a new era in his life from the reading of a book!" Of course, no serious reader would ever question whether or not books have influenced him or her— the only question would be which books and how much of an effect they'd had.

But the extent to which books can be influential goes well beyond the individual reader—they can affect society and the world as a whole. Consider, for example, the roles played in our history by such books as Tom Paine's *Common Sense*, Harriet Beecher Stowe's *Uncle Tom's Cabin*, or, more recently, Rachel Carson's *Silent Spring*, among many others.

Perhaps the greatest measure of the extent to which books can influence people is the lengths to which those who wish to restrict the freedom of others will go in trying to keep all but approved books from being read. Think of the Nazis burning books by Jewish authors, the Soviets keeping dissidents from publishing their work, or Creationists making efforts to ban Darwin's *On the Origin of Species.*

If, in fact, anyone were to question exactly how much of an influence books can have, it would be well to remember, as Thomas Bartholin wrote more than three hundred years ago, that "without books, God is silent, justice dormant, natural science at a stand, philosophy lame, letters dumb, and all things involved in darkness."

A man's life each day depends for its solidity and value on whether he reads during that day, and, far more still, on what he reads during it.

MATTHEW ARNOLD, *Culture and Anarchy* (1869)

It was books that taught me that the things that torment me most were the very things that connected me with all the people who were alive, or who had ever been alive.

JAMES BALDWIN, in *The New York Times,* January 1, 1964

The printing-press is either the greatest blessing or the greatest curse of modern times, one sometimes forgets which.

JAMES M. BARRIE, *Sentimental Tommy* (1896)

Without books, God is silent, justice dormant, natural science at a stand, philosophy lame, letters dumb, and all things involved in darkness.

THOMAS V. BARTHOLIN, "De Libris Legendis," *Dissertations* (1672) [See Barbara Tuchman, p. 54]

Some books . . . being calculated for the intellects of a few, can please only a few; yet, if they produce this effect, they answer all the end the authors intended; and if those few be men of any note, which is generally the case, the herd of mankind will very willingly fall in with their judgment, and consent to admire what they do not understand.

JAMES BEATTIE, in a letter to Sir William Forbes, May 4, 1770, in *The Life and Writings of James Beattie* by Sir William Forbes (1824)

Without books we might be tempted to believe that our civilization was born yesterday—or when the latest newsmagazine went to press. The very omnipresence of books leads us to underestimate their power and influence.

DANIEL J. BOORSTIN, *Books in Our Future* (1984)

Do you want to get at new ideas? Read old books. Do you want to find old ideas? Read new ones.

EDWARD BULWER-LYTTON, in the *Times Literary Supplement*, October 19, 1906

Laws die, Books never.

EDWARD BULWER-LYTTON, *Richelieu* (1839)

The pen is mightier than the sword.

EDWARD BULWER-LYTTON, *Richelieu* (1839)

The practice of fiction can be dangerous; it puts ideas into the head of the world.

ANTHONY BURGESS, *You've Had Your Time* (1990)

What literature can and should do is change the people who teach the people who don't buy the books.

A. S. BYATT, in *Newsweek*, June 5, 1995

Wondrous indeed is the virtue of a true Book! Not like a dead city of stones, yearly crumbling, yearly needing repair; more like a . . . spiritual tree . . . it stands from year to year, and from age to age . . . and yearly comes its new produce of leaves.

THOMAS CARLYLE, *Sartor Resartus* (1838)

The diffusion of these silent teachers, books, through the whole community, is to work greater effects than artillery, machinery, and legislation. Its peaceful agency is to supersede stormy revolutions. The culture, which is to spread, whilst an unspeakable good to the individual, is also to become the stability of nations.

WILLIAM ELLERY CHANNING, *Self-Culture* (1838)

Where books are preserved, studied and revered, human beings will also be treated with respect and dignity, and liberty will be strengthened.

WILLIAM JEFFERSON CLINTON, in a speech at the dedication of the University of Connecticut's Thomas J. Dodd Research Center, in *The New York Times,* October 16, 1995

A Book may be as great a thing as a Battle, and there are systems of Philosophy that have produced as great

Revolutions as any that have disturbed the social and political existence of our centuries.

BENJAMIN DISRAELI, in *The Calamities and Quarrels of Authors* by Isaac D'Israeli (1859)

Oh, I suppose not. Only, which three books would you have taken?

DAVID DUNCAN, *The Time Machine* (screenplay) (1960); James Filby's (Alan Young) response to a question about whether or not it mattered which three books H. G. Wells (Rod Taylor) had taken back to the future to help the Eloi rebuild civilization

We become so used to having the famous books around, most of the time we look at them as though they were statues of generals in public parks.

GEORGE P. ELLIOT, *Wonder for Huckleberry Finn* (1958)

Men of power have no time to read; yet the men who do not read are unfit for power.

MICHAEL FOOT, *Debts of Honour* (1981)

I suggest that the only books that influence us are those for which we are ready, and which have gone a

little further down our particular path than we have
yet got ourselves.

E. M. FORSTER, "A Book That Influenced Me,"
Two Cheers for Democracy (1951)

The use of letters is the principal circumstance that
distinguishes a civilized people from a herd of savages
incapable of knowledge and reflection.

EDWARD GIBBON, *The History of the Decline and Fall of the
Roman Empire* (1776–1778)

The novel, in its best form, I regard as one of the most
powerful engines of civilization ever invented.

SIR JOHN FREDERICK WILLIAM HERSCHEL, in a
speech to the subscribers of the Windsor Public Library, c. 1860

The foolishest book is a kind of leaky boat on the sea of
wisdom; some of the wisdom will get in, anyhow.

OLIVER WENDELL HOLMES, SR., *The Poet at the
Breakfast-Table* (1872)

Behold a book. I will nourish with it five thousand
souls—a million souls—all humanity. In the action of
Christ bringing forth the loaves, there is Gutenberg

bringing forth books. One sower heralds the other. . . .
Gutenberg is forever the auxiliary of life; he is the
permanent fellow-workman in the great work of
civilization. Nothing is done without him. He has marked
the transition of the man-slave to the free man.

VICTOR HUGO

Past and present, it is all the same, books are
necromancers, they exercise an influence more varied,
more lasting, than any magic known to man.

HOLBROOK JACKSON, *The Anatomy of Bibliomania* (1930)

Books are, in one sense, the basis of all social progress.

KARL MARX

Literature, well or ill conducted, is the Great Engine by
which all civilized states must ultimately be supported
or overthrown.

T. J. MATHIAS, *The Pursuits of Literature* (1794)

If good books did good, the world would have been
converted long ago.

GEORGE MOORE

$\mathbb{A}$ book, like a person, has its fortunes with one; is lucky or unlucky in its falling in our way, and often by some happy accident counts with us for something more than its independent value; [for from particular books] come subtle influences which give stability to character and help to give a man a sane outlook on the complex problems of life.

WALTER PATER, *Marius the Epicurean* (1885)

$\mathbb{W}$hile we pay lip service to the virtues of reading, the truth is that there is still in our culture something that suspects those who read too much, whatever reading too much means, of being lazy, aimless dreamers, people who need to grow up and come outside to where real life is, who think themselves superior in their separateness.

ANNA QUINDLEN, *How Reading Changed My Life* (1998)

$\mathbb{R}$eading made Don Quixote a gentleman, but believing what he read made him mad.

GEORGE BERNARD SHAW

$\mathbb{H}$ow many a man has dated a new era in his life from the reading of a book! The book exists for us perchance which will explain our miracles and reveal new ones.

HENRY DAVID THOREAU, "Reading," *Walden* (1854)

The Influence of Books

Books are the treasured wealth of the world and the fit inheritance of generations and nations. . . . Their authors are a natural and irresistible aristocracy in every society, and more than kings or emperors, exert an influence on mankind.

HENRY DAVID THOREAU, "Reading," *Walden* (1854)

Books . . . which even make us dangerous to existing institutions—such call I good books.

HENRY DAVID THOREAU, "Sunday," *A Week on the Concord and Merrimack Rivers* (1849)

Books are the carriers of civilization. Without books, history is silent, literature dumb, science crippled, thought and speculation at a standstill. They are engines of change, windows on the world, "lighthouses" as a poet said "erected in the sea of time."

BARBARA TUCHMAN, in the *Washington Post, February* 7, 1989 [See Thomas V. Bartholin, p. 47]

Literature becomes free institutions. It is the graceful ornament of civil liberty, and a happy restraint on the asperities which political controversies sometimes occasion.

DANIEL WEBSTER, in a speech in Plymouth, Massachusetts, December 22, 1820

The books that the world calls immoral are books that show the world its own shame.

OSCAR WILDE, *The Picture of Dorian Gray* (1891)

I know of no person so perfectly disagreeable and even dangerous as an author.

KING WILLIAM IV, in *Dickens' Fur Coat and Charlotte's Unanswered Letters* by Daniel Pool (1997)

The Influence of Books

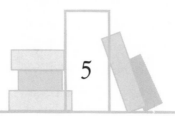

5

$\mathcal{B}$*ibliomania*

ALTHOUGH WE KNOW OF several individuals who have been credited with coining the word *bibliomania,* according to the *Oxford English Dictionary* its first use, at least in English, was by Thomas Frognall Dibdin in the title of his 1809 book, *The Bibliomania or Book Madness.*

Nearly two hundred years later, Maurice Dunbar defined a *bibliomaniac* as "a victim of the obsessive-compulsive neurosis characterized by a congested library and an atrophied bank account," contrasting this afflicted individual with a *bibliophile,* whom he defined as "a book lover . . . a victim of a markedly less acute and debilitating condition." About halfway between Dibdin and Dunbar in time, Gustave Mouravit put it more succinctly: "The bibliophile," he said, "possesses books; the bibliomane is possessed by them."

Of course, those of us who are afflicted with either bibliomania or the less virulent bibliophilia need no definition—we know the signs and symptoms only too well. We understand what James Logan meant when he said "Books are my disease," and what Desiderius Erasmus was talking about when he wrote "When I get a little money, I buy books; and if any is left, I buy food and clothes."

———

She is too fond of books, and it has turned her brain.

LOUISA MAY ALCOTT

Your ardent Bibliophile cannot pass a secondhand bookstall; he will cross the street, or go down a pestilential-looking alley, and grope among rags and dirt and filth to gratify his all-consuming passion.

ANONYMOUS

[**B**ook collecting] is a curious mania instantly understood by every other collector and almost incomprehensible to the uncontaminated.

LOUIS AUCHINCLOSS, *A Writer's Capital* (1974)

No subtle manager or broker ever saw through a maze of financial embarrassments half so quick as a poor book-buyer sees his way clear to pay for what he *must* have. He promises with himself marvels of retrenchment; he will eat less, or less costly viands, that he may buy more food for the mind. He will take an extra patch, and go on with his raiment another year, and buy books instead of coats. Yea, he will write books, that he may buy books! The appetite is insatiable. Feeding does not satisfy it. It rages by the fuel which is put upon it.

HENRY WARD BEECHER, *Star Papers; or, Experiences of Art and Nature* (1855)

Where is human nature so weak as in the bookstore!

HENRY WARD BEECHER, *Star Papers; or, Experiences of Art and Nature* (1855)

The bibliophile is the master of his books, the bibliomaniac their slave.

HANNS BOHATTA [See Gustave Mouravit, p. 65]

That lust for books which rages in the breast like a demon, and which cannot be stilled save by the frequent and plentiful acquisition of books. This passion is more common, and more powerful, than most people suppose.

Book lovers are thought by unbookish people to be gentle and unworldly, and perhaps a few of them are so. But there are others who will lie and scheme and steal to get books as wildly and unconscionably as the dope-taker in pursuit of his drug. They may not want the books to read immediately, or at all; they want them to possess, to range on their shelves, to have at command. They want books as a Turk is thought to want concubines—not to be hastily deflowered, but to be kept at their master's call, and enjoyed more often in thought than in reality.

ROBERTSON DAVIES, *Tempest-Tost* (1951)

"I will frankly confess," rejoined Lysander, "that I am an arrant bibliomaniac—that I love books dearly—that the very sight, touch, and mere perusal—"

"Hold, my friend," again exclaimed Philemon; "you have renounced your profession—you talk of reading books—do bibliomaniacs ever *read* books?"

THOMAS FROGNALL DIBDIN, *The Bibliomania or Book Madness* (1809)

Bibliomania, or the collecting of an enormous heap of books without intelligent curiosity, has, since libraries have existed, infected weak minds, who imagine that they themselves acquire knowledge when they keep it on their shelves.

ISAAC D'ISRAELI, "The Bibliomania," *Curiosities of Literature* (1791–1834)

Bibliomaniac: A victim of the obsessive-compulsive neurosis characterized by a congested library and an atrophied bank account.

MAURICE DUNBAR, *Hooked on Books* (1997)

When I get a little money, I buy books; and if any is left, I buy food and clothes.

DESIDERIUS ERASMUS [See John Lyly, p. 64; Tom Raabe, p. 66; and Robert Southey, p. 66]

A wolfish, insatiable hunger for printed paper and reading matter is the scourge of our civilization.

GUGLIELMO FERRERO, *Ancient Rome and Modern America* (1914)

What wild desires, what restless torments seize
The hapless man, who feels the book-disease.

DR. JOHN FERRIAR, "The Bibliomania: An Epistle to Richard Heber, Esq." (1863)

I have no mistress but my books.

S. J. ADAIR FITZGERALD, "My Books," *Book-Song*

"And why," I asked myself, "why should I have learned that this precious book exists, if I am never to possess it—never even to see it?" I would go to seek it in the burning heart of Africa, or in the icy regions of the Pole if I knew where it were there. But I do not know where it is. I do not know if it be guarded in a triple-locked iron case by some jealous bibliomaniac. I do not know if it be growing mouldy in the attic of some ignoramus. I shudder at the thought that perhaps its torn-out leaves may have been used to cover the pickle-jars of some housekeeper.

ANATOLE FRANCE, *The Crime of Sylvestre Bonnard* (1881)

There is no true love without some sensuality. One is not happy in books unless one loves to caress them.

ANATOLE FRANCE, *On Life and Letters* (1914)

[Bibliomania] seizes hold of rational beings, and so perverts them that in the sufferer's mind the human race exists for the sake of the books, and not the books for the sake of the human race.

FREDERIC HARRISON, *The Choice of Books and Other Literary Pieces* (1886)

No gentleman can comfortably do without three copies of a book. One he must have for his show copy, and he will probably keep it in his country house. Another he will require for his own use and reference; and unless he is inclined to part with this, which is very inconvenient, or risk the injury of his best copy, he must have a third copy at the service of his friends.

RICHARD HEBER

When I want a book, it is as a tiger wants a sheep. I must have it with one spring, and, if I miss it, go away defeated and hungry.

OLIVER WENDELL HOLMES, SR., *The Poet at the Breakfast-Table* (1872)

There is no greater cause of bibliomania than bibliophilia inordinately pursued, no better cure than study or adventurous and eventful reading.

HOLBROOK JACKSON, *The Anatomy of Bibliomania* (1930)

Books are my disease.

JAMES LOGAN, in *The Library of James Logan* by Edwin Wolf II (1974)

[It is] far more seemly to have thy Studie full of Bookes, than thy Purse full of money.

JOHN LYLY, *Euphues* (1579) [See Desiderius Erasmus, p. 61; Tom Raabe, p. 66; and Robert Southey, p. 66]

[T]here are a lot of people like me, people who need books the way they need air.

RICHARD MAREK, *Works of Genius* (1987)

There are some people . . . who are constantly drunk on books, as other men are drunk on whiskey or religion. They wander through this most diverting and stimulating of worlds in a haze, seeing nothing and hearing nothing.

H. L. MENCKEN, *Minority Report: H. L. Mencken's Notebooks* (1956)

Bibliomania, the passionate desire to handle, possess and accumulate books, has been the subject of warnings by many writers, mostly those who have been touched by it themselves. Others, however, have defended it on the grounds that, since as one grows older one's level of insanity inevitably increases, it is best to adopt one of the more liberal forms of madness such as obsession with books.

JOHN MICHELL, *Eccentric Lives and Peculiar Notions* (1984)

But whether it be worth or looks
We gently love or strongly,
Such virtue doth reside in books
We scarce can love them wrongly.

<small>COSMO MONKHOUSE</small>, "De Libris," in *Book-Song*

The bibliophile possesses books; the bibliomane is
possessed by them.

<small>GUSTAVE MOURAVIT</small>, *Le Livre et la Petite Bibliothèque
d'Amateur* (1870) [See Hanns Bohatta, p. 59]

A bibliophile of little means is likely to suffer often.
Books don't slip from his hands but fly past him through
the air, high as birds, high as prices.

<small>PABLO NERUDA</small>, *Memoirs* (1974)

One unquenchable longing has the mastery of me,
which hitherto I neither would nor could repress; 'tis an
insatiable craving for books, although, perhaps, I already
have more than I ought.

<small>FRANCESCO PETRARCH</small>, in *Francesco Petrarca* by
E. H. R. Tatham

Bibliomania

Tough choices face the biblioholic at every step of the way—like choosing between reading and eating, between buying new clothes and buying books, between a reasonable lifestyle and one of penurious but masochistic happiness lived out in the wallow of excess.

TOM RAABE, *Biblioholism: The Literary Addiction* (1991)
[See Desiderius Erasmus, p. 61; John Lyly, p. 64; and Robert Southey, below]

I have known men to hazard their fortunes, go long journeys halfway about the world, forget friendships, even lie, cheat, and steal, all for the gain of a book.

A.S.W. ROSENBACH, *Books and Bidders* (1927)

[Books are] not only the pride of my eye, and the joy of my heart, and the food of my mind, but more than metaphorically, meat, drink and clothes for me and mine.

ROBERT SOUTHEY [See Desiderius Erasmus, p. 61; John Lyly, p. 64; and Tom Raabe, above]

6

The Pleasures of Reading

HOW DOES ONE EXPRESS the pleasures of reading? How do we communicate the myriad joys to be had from the seemingly simple act of opening a book and delving into its pages? Over the centuries there have been many who have tried to do so, albeit with varying degrees of success.

It has been said that reading is a "selfish, serene, life-long intoxication," "a great gift," "a moral illumination," "more sweet, more gracious, more elevating, and more fortifying" than any other activity. It's also been called "intimate converse with men of unseen generations," "my home, my sustenance, my great invincible companion," and a "pleasure without compare." Perhaps Thomas B. Macaulay came closest to exemplifying the true pleasures of reading when he wrote "I would rather be a poor man in a garret with plenty of books than a king who did not love reading."

But ultimately the pleasure each of us derives from reading is a very personal one, and one that, despite the efforts of all those who have tried to define it for us, we must all define for ourselves.

Of all the diversions of life, there is none so proper to fill up its empty spaces as the reading of useful and entertaining authors.

JOSEPH ADDISON, in *The Spectator,* June 16, 1711

People read for amusement. If a book be capable of yielding amusement, it will naturally be read; for no man is an enemy to what gives him pleasure.

JAMES BEATTIE, in a letter to Sir William Forbes, May 4, 1770, in *The Life and Writings of James Beattie* by Sir William Forbes (1824)

Of all the human relaxations which are free from guilt, [there are] none so dignified as reading.

SIR SAMUEL EGERTON BRYDGES, *The Ruminator* (1813)

I do not know that I am happiest when alone; but this I am sure of, that I am never long even in the company of her I love without a yearning for the company of my lamp and my utterly confused and tumbled-over library.

GEORGE GORDON, LORD BYRON

Due attention to the inside of books, and due contempt for the outside, is the proper relation between a man of sense and his books.

PHILIP DORMER STANHOPE, EARL OF CHESTERFIELD, *Letters to His Son* (1774)

Man has no amusement more innocent, more sweet, more gracious, more elevating, and more fortifying than he can find in a library.

GEORGE DAWSON, in a speech at the opening of the Birmingham Free Reference Library, 1866

The good of a book lies in its being read. A book is made up of signs that speak of other signs, which in turn speak of things.

UMBERTO ECO, *The Name of the Rose* (1981)

Ah! The books that one will never read again: they gave delight, perchance something more; they left a perfume in the memory; but life has passed them by forever.

GEORGE GISSING, *The Private Papers of Henry Ryecroft* (1903)

A well-composed book is a magic carpet on which we are wafted to a world that we cannot enter in any other way.

CAROLINE GORDON

What a convenient and delightful world is this world of books!—if you bring to it not the obligations of the student, or look upon it as an opiate for idleness, but enter it rather with the enthusiasm of the adventurer!

DAVID GRAYSON, *Adventures in Contentment* (1907)

Without having acquired the power of reading for pleasure none of us can be independent.

EDWARD, VISCOUNT GREY OF FALLODON, "Recreation," *Fallodon Papers* (1926)

When I open a noble volume I say to myself, "Now the only Croesus that I envy is he who is reading a better book than this."

PHILIP GILBERT HAMERTON, *The Intellectual Life* (1873)

The great gift is a passion for reading. It is cheap, it consoles, it distracts, it excites, it gives you knowledge of the world and experience of a wide kind. It is a moral illumination.

ELIZABETH HARDWICK

In a very real sense, people who have read good literature have lived more than people who cannot or will not read. . . . It is not true that we have only one life to live; if we can read, we can live as many more lives and as many kinds of lives as we wish.

S. I. HAYAKAWA

Woe be to him that reads but one book.

GEORGE HERBERT, *Jacula Prudentum* (1651)

If I were to pray for a taste which should stand me in stead under every variety of circumstances, and be a source of happiness and cheerfulness to me through life, and a shield against its ills, however things might go amiss, and the world frown upon me, it would be a taste for reading. . . . Give a man this taste, and the means of gratifying it, and you can hardly fail of making a happy man. . . . You place him in contact with the best society in every period of history—with the wisest, the wittiest—with the tenderest, the bravest, and the purest characters who have adorned humanity. You make him a denizen of all nations—a contemporary of all ages. The world has been created for him.

SIR JOHN FREDERICK WILLIAM HERSCHEL, in a speech to the subscribers of the Windsor Public Library, c. 1860 [See Robert Lowe, Lord Sherbrooke, p. 77]

What we read with pleasure we read again with pleasure.

HORACE

Reading is not a duty, and if it is not a pleasure it is a waste of time.

HOLBROOK JACKSON, *The Anatomy of Bibliomania* (1930)

Take thou a book in thine hands. . . . And when thou hast finished reading, close the book and give thanks for every word out of the mouth of God; because in the Lord's field thou hast found a hidden treasure.

THOMAS À KEMPIS

To sit alone in the lamplight with a book spread out before you, and hold intimate converse with men of unseen generations—such is a pleasure beyond compare.

YOSHIDA KENKO, *Essays in Idleness* (1688)

How beautiful to a genuine lover of reading are the sullied leaves and worn-out appearance, nay the very odour . . . of an old "Circulating library" *Tom Jones* or *Vicar of Wakefield*. How they speak of the thousand thumbs that have turned over their pages with delight.

CHARLES LAMB, "Detached Thoughts on Books and Reading," *Essays of Elia* (1823)

What is reading but silent conversation?

WALTER SAVAGE LANDOR, "Aristoteles and Callisthenes," *Imaginary Conversations* (1876)

Until I feared I would lose it, I never loved to read.
One does not love breathing.

HARPER LEE, *To Kill a Mockingbird* (1960)

Have you ever rightly considered what the mere ability
to read means? That it is the key which admits us to the
whole world of thought and fancy and imagination? To
the company of saint and sage, of the wisest and the
wittiest at their wisest and wittiest moment? That it
enables us to see with the keenest eyes, hear with the
finest ears, and listen to the sweetest voices of all time?

JAMES RUSSELL LOWELL, "Books and Libraries,"
Democracy and Other Addresses (1887)

Only one hour in the normal day is more pleasurable
than the hour spent in bed with a book before going
to sleep, and that is the hour spent in bed with a book
after being called in the morning.

ROSE MACAULAY

I have no pleasure from books which equals that of
reading over for the hundredth time great productions
which I almost know by heart.

THOMAS B. MACAULAY, *The Life and Letters of Thomas B.
Macaulay*, edited by George Otto Trevelyan (1876)

Speaking of Books

I would rather be a poor man in a garret with plenty of books than a king who did not love reading.

THOMAS B. MACAULAY, *The Life and Letters of Thomas B. Macaulay,* edited by George Otto Trevelyan (1876)

The pleasure of all reading is doubled when one lives with another who shares the same books.

KATHERINE MANSFIELD, *The Letters of Katherine Mansfield,* edited by J. Middleton Murry (1928)

No entertainment is so cheap as reading, nor any pleasure so lasting. She will not want new fashions, nor regret the loss of expensive diversions, or variety of company, if she can be amused with an author in her closet.

LADY MARY WORTLEY MONTAGU, in a letter to her daughter, June 22, 1752, *The Selected Letters,* edited by Robert Halsband (1970)

I know not how to abstain from reading.

SAMUEL PEPYS, *Diary* (1893–1899)

I divide all readers into two classes: those who read to remember and those who read to forget.

WILLIAM LYON PHELPS

Reading makes immigrants of us all. It takes us away from home, but, most important, it finds homes for us everywhere.

HAZEL ROCHMAN, in *How Reading Changed My Life* by Anna Quindlen (1998)

I cannot think of a greater blessing than to die in one's own bed, without warning or discomfort, on the last page of a new book that we most wanted to read.

LORD JOHN RUSSELL

I envied my older sister her uninterruptability. While I looked up immediately from my book when my name was called, she had the uncanny ability not to hear. I would test her as she read. It was like addressing a stone, except that with a stone, if we are imaginative enough, we can infer some kind of response, albeit in stone language. My sister appeared to be present, but she was in the book. This is a great and useful gift.

The stunned petitioner retreats, daunted by an invisible power that can drown out the world.

LYNNE SHARON SCHWARTZ, *Ruined by Reading* (1996)

Cultivate above all things a taste for reading. There is no pleasure so cheap, so innocent, and so remunerative as the real, hearty pleasure and taste for reading. . . . Some people take to it naturally, and others do not; but I advise you to cultivate it, and endeavour to promote it in your minds. In order to do that you should read what amuses you and pleases you. You should not begin with difficult works, because, if you do, you will find the pursuit dry and tiresome. I would even say to you, read novels, read frivolous books, read anything that will amuse you and give you a taste for reading. On this point all persons could put themselves on an equality. Some persons would say they would rather spend their time in society; but it must be remembered that if they had cultivated a taste for reading beforehand they would be in a position to choose their society, whereas, if they had not, the probabilities were that they would have to mix with people inferior to themselves.

ROBERT LOWE, LORD SHERBROOKE, in a speech to the students of the Croydon Science and Arts School, 1869 [See Sir John Frederick William Herschel, p. 72]

The nice and subtle happiness of reading . . . this joy not dulled by age, this polite and unpunished vice, this selfish, serene, life-long intoxication.

LOGAN PEARSALL SMITH, *Trivia* (1918)

Reading is to the mind what exercise is to the body. As by the one health is preserved, strengthened, and invigorated; by the other, virtue (which is the health of the mind) is kept alive, cherished, and confirmed.

SIR RICHARD STEELE, *The Tatler*, March 18, 1710

[There is] full as much pleasure in reading a very excellent book the fifth or sixth time, as if one had it fresh from the press.

CATHERINE TALBOT

Book love: It will make your hours pleasant as long as you live.

ANTHONY TROLLOPE

Of all the needs a book has the chief need is that it be readable.

ANTHONY TROLLOPE, *Autobiography* (1883)

I have sometimes dreamt . . . that when the Day of Judgment dawns and the great conquerors and lawyers and statesmen come to receive their awards . . . the Almighty will . . . say, not without a certain envy when He sees us coming with our books under our arms, "Look, these need no reward. We have nothing to give them here. They have loved reading."

VIRGINIA WOOLF, *The Common Reader* (1925)

Dreams, books, are each a world; and books, we know,
Are a substantial world, both pure and good:
Round these, with tendrils strong as flesh and blood,
Our pastime and our happiness will grow.

WILLIAM WORDSWORTH, *Personal Talk* (1807)

Twice five years
Or less I might have seen, when first my mind
With conscious pleasure opened to the charm
Of words in tuneful order, found them sweet
For their own sakes, a passion, and a power;
And phrases pleased me chosen for delight,
For pomp, or love.

WILLIAM WORDSWORTH, *The Prelude* (1850)

7

What Books Do~and Don't Do~For Us

AS BOOK LOVERS, indeed, as literate individuals, we take it for granted that we can gain a great deal from books, that they provide us with a range of benefits unlike any we can find elsewhere. Books can provide counsel, friendship, comfort, and knowledge. They can provide pleasure, romance, excitement, and, sometimes, even wisdom. In the pages that follow you will find many who readily attest to this.

There are others, however, who introduce a cautionary note, who warn us that we can grow too dependent on books. They remind us that, for all the benefits we can derive from books, and although we may tend to see them as such, they are not a panacea.

As Oliver Wendell Holmes, Sr., put it, "I always believed in life rather than books."

It would be easy to think of these positions as representing two opposing camps, but the truth is probably more complicated. Taking both sides into account, we would probably be well advised to take to heart William Hazlitt's suggestion: "Books are a world in themselves, it is true; but they are not the only world. The world itself is a volume larger than all the libraries in it."

A real book is not one that's read, but one that reads us.

W. H. AUDEN, recalled on his death, September 28, 1973

Reading maketh a full man; conference a ready man; and writing an exact man.

FRANCIS BACON, "Of Studies," *Essays* (1625)

Books will speak plain when counsellors blanch.

FRANCIS BACON, "Of Counsel," *Essays* (1625)

Books say: she did this because. Life says: she did this. Books are where things are explained to you; life is where things aren't. . . . Books make sense of life. The only problem is that the lives they make sense of are other people's lives, never your own.

JULIAN BARNES, *Flaubert's Parrot* (1984)

He that loveth a book will never want a faithful friend.

ISAAC BARROW, "Of Industry in Our Particular Calling as Scholars," *The Works* (1683)

The man who adds the life of books to the actual life of everyday lives the life of the whole race. The man without books lives only the life of one individual.

JESSIE LEE BENNETT, *What Books Can Do for You* (1923)

The failure to read good books both enfeebles the vision and strengthens our most fatal tendency—the belief that here and now is all there is.

ALLAN BLOOM, *The Closing of the American Mind* (1987)

A book to me means love because when you give a book about a romantic place it's like saying that all the days of your life should be as romantic as Spain and surrounded by a cover of happiness.

JOSEPH BOLOGNA, DAVID ZELAG GOODMAN, AND RENEE TAYLOR, *Lovers and Other Strangers* (screenplay) (1970)

[Books are] the assembled souls of all that men held wise, imprisoned until some one takes them down from a shelf and reads them.

SAMUEL BUTLER, *The Note-Books of Samuel Butler,* edited by Henry Festing Jones (1912)

It is chiefly through books that we enjoy intercourse with superior minds. . . . In the best books, great men talk to us, give us their most precious thoughts, and pour their souls into ours. God be thanked for Books! They are the voices of the distant and the dead, and make us heirs of the spiritual life of past ages. Books are the true levellers. They give to all, who will faithfully use them, the society, the spiritual presence, of the best and greatest of our race.

WILLIAM ELLERY CHANNING, *Self-Culture* (1838)

No matter how poor I am. No matter though the prosperous of my own time will not enter my obscure dwelling. If the Sacred Writers will enter and take up their abode under my roof, if Milton will cross my threshold to sing to me of Paradise, and Shakespeare to open to me the worlds of imagination and the workings of the human heart, and Franklin to enrich me with his practical wisdom, I shall not pine for want of intellectual companionship, and I may become a cultivated man, though excluded from what is called the best society in the place where I live.

WILLIAM ELLERY CHANNING, *Self-Culture* (1838)

Take away the art of writing from this world, and you will probably take away its glory.

FRANÇOIS RENÉ DE CHATEAUBRIAND,
Les Natchez (1826)

Some read to think, these are rare; some to write, these are common; and some read to talk, and these form the great majority. The first page of an author not unfrequently suffices for all the purposes of this later class: of whom it has been said, that they treat books as some do lords; they inform themselves of their *titles*, and then boast of an intimate acquaintance.

CHARLES CALEB COLTON, *Lacon: or, Many Things in Few Words; Addressed to Those Who Think* (1823)

[Books are] wells of living waters, delightful ears of corn, combs of honey, golden pots in which manna is stored, and udders of milk.

RICHARD DE BURY, *Philobiblon* (1473)

In books I find the dead as if they were alive; in books I foresee things to come; in books warlike affairs are set forth; from books come forth the laws of peace. All things are corrupted and decay in time; . . . all the glory of the world would be buried in oblivion, unless God had provided mortals with the remedy of books.

RICHARD DE BURY, *Philobiblon* (1473)

The reading of all good books is like conversation with the finest men of past centuries.

RENÉ DESCARTES, *Discourse on Method* (1637)

There is no Frigate like a Book
To take us Lands away
Nor any Coursers like a Page
Of prancing Poetry.

EMILY DICKINSON, "A Book (2)," *Poems,*
Third Series (1896)

Books are the quietest and most constant of friends; they are the most accessible and wisest of counselors, and the most patient of teachers.

CHARLES W. ELIOT, *The Happy Life* (1896)

[**T**he best service of books is] that they set us free from themselves. We read a line, a word, that lifts us; we rise into a succession of thoughts that is better than the book.

RALPH WALDO EMERSON, *Journals,* edited by Edward Waldo Emerson and Waldo Emerson Forbes (1914)

It seemed to me as if I had written the book myself in some former life, so sincerely it spoke my thought and experience.

RALPH WALDO EMERSON, on reading Montaigne, *Journals,* edited by Edward Waldo Emerson and Waldo Emerson Forbes (1914) [See Clifton Fadiman, p. 88; A. W. and J. C. Hare, p. 89; and Edmund Wilson, p. 96]

Some books leave us free and some books make us free.

RALPH WALDO EMERSON, *Journals,* edited by Edward Waldo Emerson and Waldo Emerson Forbes (1914)

What Books Do—and Don't Do—For Us

The profit of books is according to the sensibility of the reader; the profoundest thought or passion sleeps as in a mine, until it is discovered by an equal mind and heart.

RALPH WALDO EMERSON, "Success," *Society and Solitude* (1870)

When you re/read a classic you do not see more in the book than you did before; you see more in *you* than there was before.

CLIFTON FADIMAN, *Any Number Can Play* (1957) [See Ralph Waldo Emerson, p. 87; A. W. and J. C. Hare, p. 89; and Edmund Wilson, p. 96]

Read in order to Live.

GUSTAVE FLAUBERT, in a letter to Mademoiselle de Chantepic, June 1857

I am not able to fall asleep without reading. You have that time when your brain has nothing constructive to do so it rambles. I fool my brain out of that by making it read until it shuts off.

KAYE GIBBONS, *Ellen Foster* (1987)

Books do not make life easier or more simple, but harder and more interesting.

HARRY GOLDEN, *So What Else Is New* (1964)

When a man says he sees nothing in a book, he very often means that he does not see himself in it.

A. W. AND J. C. HARE, *Guesses at Truth* (1827) [See Ralph Waldo Emerson, p. 87; Clifton Fadiman, p. 88; and Edmund Wilson, p. 96)

The book-lover needs most to be reminded that man's business here is to know for the sake of living, not to live for the sake of knowing.

FREDERIC HARRISON, *The Choice of Books and Other Literary Pieces* (1886)

Books are a world in themselves, it is true; but they are not the only world. The world itself is a volume larger than all the libraries in it.

WILLIAM HAZLITT, "Of the Conversation of Authors," *The Plain Speaker* (1826)

A few good books, digested well, do feed
The mind; much clogs, or doth ill humours breed.

D. HEATH, *Praise of Books*

Journalism allows its readers to witness history;
fiction gives its readers an opportunity to live it.

JOHN HERSEY, in *Time,* March 13, 1950

The reading animal will not be content with the brutish
wallowings that satisfy the unlearned pigs of the world.

THOMAS HOOD, in a letter to the Manchester
Athenaeum, 1843

I cannot comment on the "meaning or purpose of life."
I am a novelist, not a philosopher, and while all novels
set out to answer the question of the meaning of life,
only the bad ones succeed.

WILLIAM HUMPHREY, in a book proposal for
The Meaning of Life by Hugh S. Morehead, 1989

[Our world is] divisible into two worlds: the common
geographical world, and the world of books . . . [which
are] such real things that if habit and perception make

the difference between real and unreal, we may say that we more frequently wake out of common life to them, than out of them to common life.

LEIGH HUNT, in *Monthly Repository*, 1828

The right book annihilates time.

HOLBROOK JACKSON, *The Anatomy of Bibliomania* (1930)

If we are imprisoned in ourselves, books provide us with the means of escape. If we have run too far away from ourselves, books show us the way back.

HOLBROOK JACKSON, *Maxims of Books and Reading* (1934)

I cannot live without books.

THOMAS JEFFERSON, in a letter to John Adams, June 10, 1815

Some read that they may embellish their conversation, or shine in dispute; some that they may not be detected in ignorance, or want the reputation of literary accomplishments; but the most general and prevalent reason of study is the impossibility of finding another amusement equally cheap or constant, equally independent of the hour or the weather.

DR. SAMUEL JOHNSON, in *The Adventurer,* 1753–1754

Books have always a secret influence on the understanding: we cannot at pleasure obliterate ideas; he that reads books of science, though without any fixed desire of improvement, will grow more knowing; he that entertains himself with moral or religious treatises will imperceptibly advance in goodness; the ideas which are often offered to the mind will at last find a lucky moment when it is disposed to receive them.

DR. SAMUEL JOHNSON, in *The Adventurer,* 1753–1754

I love to lose myself in other men's minds. When I am not walking, I am reading; I cannot sit and think. Books think for me.

CHARLES LAMB, "Detached Thoughts on Books and Reading," *Last Essays of Elia* (1833)

A book is a friend whose face is constantly changing.

ANDREW LANG, *The Library* (1881)

A book is a mirror: if an ass peers into it, you can't expect an apostle to look out.

GEORG CHRISTOPH LICHTENBERG, *Aphorisms* (1764–1799)

The many books he read but served to whet his unrest. Every page of every book was a peep-hole into the realm of knowledge. His hunger fed upon what he read, and increased.

JACK LONDON, *Martin Eden* (1909)

All books are either dreams or swords.
You can cut, or you can drug, with words.

AMY LOWELL, "Sword Blades and Poppy Seeds," *Sword Blades and Poppy Seeds* (1914)

For whatever is truly wondrous and fearful in man, never yet was put into words or books.

HERMAN MELVILLE, *Moby-Dick* (1851)

A man loses contact with reality if he is not surrounded by his books.

FRANÇOIS MITTERRAND, President of France, in the [London] *Times*, May 10, 1982

When you sell a man a book you don't sell just twelve ounces of paper and ink and glue—you sell him a whole new life. Love and friendship and humour and ships at sea by night—there's all heaven and earth in a book, a real book.

CHRISTOPHER MORLEY

Seek in literature deliverance from mortality.

PLINY, in *Marius the Epicurean* by Walter Pater (1885)

Life deceives us so much that we come to believing that literature has no relation with it and are astonished to observe that the wonderful ideas books have presented to us are gratuitously exhibited in everyday life, without risk of being spoilt by the writer.

MARCEL PROUST

The companionship of books is unquestionably one of the greatest antidotes to the ravages of time, and study is better than all medical formulas for the prolongation of life.

WILLIAM ROBERTS, *The Book-Hunter in London* (1895)

Literature is the one place in any society where, within the secrecy of our own heads, we can hear voices talking about everything in every possible way.

SALMAN RUSHDIE, *Is Nothing Sacred?* (1990)

If public libraries were half as costly as public dinners, or books cost the tenth part of what bracelets do, even foolish men and women might sometimes suspect there was good in reading, as well as in munching and sparkling.

JOHN RUSKIN, *Sesame and Lilies* (1865)

We talk of food for the mind, as of food for the body: now a good book contains such food inexhaustibly; it is a provision for life, and for the best part of us.

JOHN RUSKIN, *Sesame and Lilies* (1865)

As meat to the body, so is reading to the soul.

SENECA

A great book should leave you with many experiences, and slightly exhausted at the end. You live several lives while reading it.

WILLIAM STYRON, in *Writers at Work—First Series,* edited by Malcolm Cowley (1958)

Great writers are not those who tell us we shouldn't play with fire but those who make our fingers burn.

STEPHEN VIZINCZEY, *Truth and Lies in Literature* (1986)

No two people read the same book.

EDMUND WILSON, in the *Sunday Times,* July 25, 1971 [See Ralph Waldo Emerson, p. 87; Clifton Fadiman, p. 88; and A. W. and J. C. Hare, p. 89]

All Those Books...

FOR THOSE OF US WHO collect—or even simply
gather—books, there is no such thing as too many books.
As Susan Sontag puts it, "The collector's need is precisely
for excess, for surfeit, for profusion. It's too much—and
it's just enough for me. . . . A collection is always more
than is necessary."

While this is always understood by other book
collectors, and often by those who collect other things—
be they porcelain figurines, compact discs, or souvenir
spoons—it is rarely understood by those who don't collect
anything. Even otherwise intelligent and sophisticated
people will sometimes, on viewing our private libraries,
be more impressed by the sheer number of volumes than
by their variety, quality, or any other measure.

For those who are less sophisticated—not to say less intelligent—our collections are sources of wonder not only because of their size but because of the fact that they are comprised of books. For such individuals, it is impossible to even imagine why anyone would want to have so many books. And this lack of imagination almost invariably leads them to ask the question we have all heard so many times: "Have you read all these books?"

Although many have suggested answers to this foolish question, we feel compelled to say that we've never heard one that we found to be entirely satisfactory. We can, and do, however, take comfort from Chaim Grade's argument that "if anyone asks you if you've read all those books, it means you don't have enough books."

I hold the buying of more books than one can peradventure read, as nothing less than the soul's reaching towards infinity; which is the only thing that raises us above the beasts that perish.

ANONYMOUS

You can never be too thin, too rich, or have too many books.

CARTER BURDEN, in *Vogue,* March 1987

That one should possess no books beyond his power of perusal—that he should buy no faster than as he can read straight through what he has already bought—is a supposition alike preposterous and unreasonable. "Surely you have far more books that you can read" is sometimes the inane remark of the barbarian who gets his books, volume by volume, from some circulating library or reading club, and reads them all through, one after the other, with a dreary dutifulness, that he may be sure that he has got the value of his money.

JOHN HILL BURTON, *The Book-Hunter* (1862)

Within the span of life allotted to man there is but a certain number of books that it is practicable to read through, and it is not possible to make a selection that will not, in a manner, wall in the mind from a free expansion over the republic of letters.

JOHN HILL BURTON, *The Book-Hunter* (1862)

If people bought no more books than they intended to read, and no more swords than they intended to use, the two worst trades in Europe would be a bookseller's and a sword-cutler's; but luckily for both they are reckoned genteel ornaments.

PHILIP DORMER STANHOPE, EARL OF CHESTERFIELD

All Those Books...

Our accountant nearly dropped dead when he saw what I spent on books last year. My husband said: "I guess he doesn't know too many people who would spend more money on books than clothes."

MICHELE OKA DONER, in *At Home with Books* by Estelle Ellis, Caroline Seebohm, and Christopher Simon Sykes (1995)

[Having moved into a new office] For the first time in my life—although doubtless not for long—I now have more bookshelves than books. That, for someone like me, is not a bad definition of heaven on earth.

JOHN STEELE GORDON, *Hamilton's Blessing* (1997)

If anyone asks you if you've read all those books, it means you don't have enough books.

CHAIM GRADE, in "They Don't Call It a Mania for Nothing" by Harold Rabinowitz, *A Passion for Books,* edited by Harold Rabinowitz and Rob Kaplan (1999)

There are 10,000 books in my library, and it will keep growing until I die. This has exasperated my daughters, amused my friends and baffled my accountant. If I had not picked up this habit in the library long ago,

I would have more money in the bank today; I would not be richer.

PETE HAMILL, "D'Artagnan on Ninth Street: A Brooklyn Boy at the Library," in *A Book Lover's Diary: The Reader's Companion* by Shelagh Wallace (1996)

What refuge is there for the victim who is oppressed with the feeling that there are a thousand new books he ought to read, while life is only long enough for him to attempt to read a hundred?

OLIVER WENDELL HOLMES, SR., *Over the Teacups* (1891)

Any man with a moderate income can afford to buy more books than he can read in a lifetime.

HENRY HOLT, in *Publishers Weekly*, September 27, 1991

If I had to choose between a wall of paintings and a wall of books, I would certainly choose books. When you walk into a room of books, you're embraced by them.

TIMOTHY MAWSON, in *At Home with Books* by Estelle Ellis, Caroline Seebohm, and Christopher Simon Sykes (1995)

Affect not as some do that bookish ambition to be stored with books and have well-furnished libraries,

yet keep their heads empty of knowledge; to desire to
have many books, and never to use them, is like a child
that will have a candle burning by him all the while
he is sleeping.

HENRY PEACHAM, *The Compleat Gentleman* (1622)

Maybe I have more than I need, but it is the same with
books as with everything else—success in finding them
spurs one on to greed for more.

FRANCESCO PETRARCH

I wish to have one copy of every book in the world.

SIR THOMAS PHILLIPPS, in *Portrait of an Obsession* by
A.N.L. Munby (1967)

I would be most content if my children grew up to be
the kind of people who think decorating consists mostly
of building enough bookshelves.

ANNA QUINDLEN, "Enough Bookshelves," *The New York
Times*, August 7, 1991

The one thing I regret is that I will never have time to read all the books I want to read.

FRANÇOISE SAGAN, in *Uncommon Scold* by Abby Adams (1989)

To buy books would be a good thing if we also could buy the time to read them. As it is, the act of purchasing them is often mistaken for the assimilation and mastering of their content.

ARTHUR SCHOPENHAUER

Of what use are books without number and complete collections, if their owner barely finds time in the course of his life to read their titles?

SENECA

When you bet on the horse race, you bet for win, for place, for show. When you buy books, you buy some to read, some to own, and some for reference. You want to possess the books, you want to own them, you want to hold them. Perhaps you even hope that you will read them.

LOUIS SZATHMARY, in *A Gentle Madness* by Nicholas A. Basbanes (1995)

Books are now multiplied to such a degree, that it is impossible not only to read them all, but even to know their number and their titles. Happily, one is not obliged to read all that is published.

VOLTAIRE, *Philosophical Dictionary* (1764)

9

How to Read

THERE ARE AT LEAST as many ways to read as there are readers. Some of us read in bed, some on our way to and/or from work. Some of us have special chairs or corners we sit in, and some can read almost anywhere. Some of us insist on floor lamps to sit under, and some the kind of lights that clamp onto the books themselves.

Moreover, while there are those who feel they must read every single word of a book before they can claim to have truly read it, there are others who are adept at the art of skimming. And, while there are some who, as a matter of principle, never read a book more than once, there are others who believe that at least some books should be read over and over until one has almost learned them by heart.

The fact that there is so much disagreement about how to read brings us to the inevitable conclusion that there is no "right" way, and that every individual must choose for him= or herself, as each of the authors who follow has done.

––––––––

Read not to contradict and confute, nor to believe and take for granted, nor to find talk and discourse; but to weigh and consider.

FRANCIS BACON, "Of Studies," *Essays* (1625)

Some books are to be tasted, others to be swallowed, and some few to be chewed and digested; that is, some books are to be read only in parts; others to be read but not curiously; and some few to be read wholly, and with diligence and attention.

FRANCIS BACON, "Of Studies," *Essays* (1625)

He has only half learned the art of reading who has not added to it the even more refined accomplishments of skipping and skimming.

LORD ARTHUR JAMES BALFOUR, in *Mr. Balfour* by E. T. Raymond (1920)

We all generally err by *reading too much,* and out of proportion to what we *think.* I should be wiser, I am persuaded, if I had not read half as much—should have had stronger and better exercised faculties, and should stand higher in my own appreciation. The fact is, that the *ne plus ultra* of intellectual indolence is this reading of books. It comes next to what the Americans call "whittling."

ELIZABETH BARRETT BROWNING, in a letter to Richard Hengist Horne, December 20, 1843, *Letters of Elizabeth Barrett Browning to Richard Hengist Horne,* edited by S. R. Townshend Mayer (1877)

I may have had to make some effort myself, at first, to learn not to read, but now it comes quite naturally to me. The secret is not refusing to look at the written words. On the contrary, you must look at them, intensely, until they disappear.

ITALO CALVINO, *If on a Winter's Night a Traveler* (1979)

A truly great book should be read in youth, again in maturity, and once more in old age, as a fine building should be seen by morning light, at noon, and by moonlight.

ROBERTSON DAVIES, *The Enthusiasms of Robertson Davies* (1989)

The great sin . . . is to assume that something that has been read once has been read forever. . . . We must not gobble a work like chocolates or olives or anchovies and think we know it forever. Nobody ever reads the same book twice.

ROBERTSON DAVIES

All good and true book-lovers practice the pleasing and improving avocation of reading in bed. . . . No book can be appreciated until it has been slept with and dreamed over.

EUGENE FIELD, *Love Affairs of a Bibliomaniac* (1896)

Browse through the library of any writer or exemplary teacher and you will find the leaves of the book dog-eared and scribbled notations in all the margins. No one interested in what an author is saying should read without pencil in hand.

HARRY GOLDEN, *So What Else Is New* (1964)

The book, if you would see anything in it, requires to be read in the clear, brown, twilight atmosphere in which it was written; if opened in the sunshine, it is apt to look exceedingly like a volume of blank pages.

NATHANIEL HAWTHORNE, *Twice-Told Tales* (1851)

To be well informed, one must read quickly a great number of merely instructive books. To be cultivated, one must read slowly and with a lingering appreciation the comparatively few books that have been written by men who lived, thought, and felt with style.

ALDOUS HUXLEY

The time to read is now, not hereafter. We must make time or miss our joy.

HOLBROOK JACKSON, *The Anatomy of Bibliomania* (1930)

One must read all writers twice—the good as well as the bad. The one will be recognized; the other, unmasked.

KARL KRAUS

When I read aloud two senses catch the idea: first I see what I read; second, I hear it, and therefore I can remember it better.

ABRAHAM LINCOLN, in *Herndon's Lincoln: The True Story of a Great Life* by William H. Herndon and Jesse W. Weik (1889)

How to Read

Who reads
Incessantly, and to his reading brings not
A spirit and judgement equal or superior
(And what he brings, what needs he elsewhere seek?)
Uncertain and unsettled still remains,
Deep-versed in books and shallow in himself.

JOHN MILTON, *Paradise Regained* (1671)

A wise man will make better use of an idle pamphlet, than a fool will do of sacred Scripture.

JOHN MILTON, *Areopagitica* (1644)

You might read all the books in the British Museum (if you could live long enough) and remain an utterly "illiterate," uneducated person; but . . . if you read ten pages of a good book, letter by letter, that is to say, with real accuracy, you are evermore in some measure an educated person.

JOHN RUSKIN, *Sesame and Lilies* (1865)

Any book that is important ought to be at once read through twice . . . because we are not in the same temper and disposition on both readings.

ARTHUR SCHOPENHAUER, "On Books and Reading," *The Art of Literature* (1818)

Books must be read as deliberately and reservedly as they are written.

HENRY DAVID THOREAU, "Reading," *Walden* (1854)

To read well—that is, to read true books in a true spirit—is a noble exercise, and one that will task the reader more than any exercise which the customs of the day esteem. It requires a training such as the athletes underwent, the steady intention almost of the whole life to this subject.

HENRY DAVID THOREAU, "Reading," *Walden* (1854)

I always begin at the left with the opening word of the sentence and read towards the right, and I recommend this method.

JAMES THURBER, in *The New York Times Book Review*, December 4, 1988

I've been reading in the tub since I was nine. I've dropped books in the water, wrecked many, and may even drown someday reading in the tub. What a wonderful way to go.

JOAN VASS, in *At Home with Books* by Estelle Ellis, Caroline Seebohm, and Christopher Simon Sykes (1995)

Learn to read slowly; all other graces
Will follow in their proper places.

w. WALKER, *The Art of Reading*

Books are to be call'd for, and supplied, on the assump‐
tion that the process of reading is not a half sleep, but,
in highest sense, an exercise, a gymnast's struggle; that
the reader is to do something for himself, must be on the
alert, must himself or herself construct indeed the poem,
argument, history, metaphysical essay—the text furnishing
the hints, the clue, the start of frame‐work. Not the book
needs so much to be the complete thing, but the reader
of the book does. That were to make a nation of supple
and athletic minds, well‐train'd, intuitive, used to depend
on themselves, and not on a few coteries of writers.

WALT WHITMAN, *Democratic Vistas* (1871)

O for a booke and a shadie nooke,
Either in‐a‐door or out,
With the greene leaves whisp'ring overhede,
Or the streete cries all about,
Where I may Reade all at my ease,
Both of the Newe and Olde,
For a jollie goode Booke whereon to looke,
Is better to me than golde.

JOHN WILSON

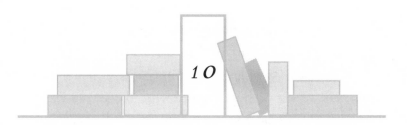

10

Libraries

IT IS IMPOSSIBLE to overemphasize the role
that libraries—particularly public libraries—have
played in fostering the love of books and reading in our
society. While bibliophiles may not regularly patronize
libraries—preferring, as many of us do, to buy and
read our own books—many, if not most of us, first
experienced that love (or those loves) in the dim recesses
of the children's section of our local library.

"The opening of a free, public library," James Russell
Lowell wrote near the end of the nineteenth century,
"is a most important event in the history of any town."
While this continues to be true in our own day, it was
even more important in Lowell's, and for all the centuries
before that. When books were largely affordable only

by people of means, it was the local public library that provided people with a place where they could taste of all the fruits of humankind's knowledge.

But libraries are more than just storehouses. To Carl Rowan they are "temples of learning," to Germaine Greer "reservoirs of strength, grace and wit." To Alexander Smith, they are places where "all history rolls before me." And to Philip Roth, the library "wasn't simply where one had to go to get the books, it was a kind of exacting haven to which a city youngster willingly went for his lesson in restraint, and his training in self-control." In fact, libraries—public and otherwise—have a different, and special, significance to everyone who visits them, as the authors on the following pages attest.

———

[Libraries] are as the shrines where all the relics of the ancient saints, full of true virtue, and that without delusion or imposture, are preserved.

FRANCIS BACON, "Of the Advancement of Learning," *Essays* (1625)

The world may be kind or unkind, it may seem to us to be hastening on the wings of enlightenment and progress to an imminent millennium, or it may weigh us down with the sense of insoluble difficulty and irremediable wrong; but whatever else it be, so long as we have good health and a good library, it can hardly be dull.

LORD ARTHUR JAMES BALFOUR, "The Pleasures of Reading," *Essays and Addresses* (1893)

I myself spent hours in the Columbia library as intimi‑dated and embarrassed as a famished gourmet invited to a dream restaurant where every dish from all the world's cuisines, past and present, was available on request.

LUIGI BARZINI, *O America* (1977)

A library is but the soul's burial‑ground. It is the land of shadows.

HENRY WARD BEECHER, *Star Papers; or, Experiences of Art and Nature* (1855)

A little library, growing larger every year, is an honourable part of a man's history. It is a man's duty to have books. A library is not a luxury, but one of the necessities of life.

HENRY WARD BEECHER, *The Sermons of Henry Ward Beecher* (1870)

I have always imagined that Paradise will be a kind of library.

JORGE LUIS BORGES

The atmosphere of libraries, lecture rooms and laboratories is dangerous to those who shut themselves up in them too long. It separates us from reality like a fog.

ALEXIS CARREL, *Reflections on Life* (1952)

Here all that live no more; preserved they lie,
In tombs that open to the curious eye.

GEORGE CRABBE, *The Library* (1781)

Beside a library, how poor are all the other greatest deeds of man.

THOMAS DAVIS, "Essay on Study" (1845)

The great consulting room of a wise man is a library. When I am in perplexity about life, I have but to come here, and, without fee or reward, I commune with the wisest souls that God has blessed the world with.

GEORGE DAWSON, in a speech at the opening of the Birmingham Free Reference Library, 1866

As in apothecaries' shops all sorts of drugs are permitted to be, so may all sorts of books be in a library. And as they out of vipers and scorpions, and poisoning vegetables, extract often wholesome medicaments, for the life of mankind; so out of whatsoever books, good instructions and examples may be acquired.

WILLIAM DRUMMOND, "Of Libraries" (c. 1625)
[See Richard le Gallienne, p. 120]

A man's library is a sort of harem.

RALPH WALDO EMERSON, "In Praise of Books,"
The Conduct of Life (1860) [See Leigh Hunt, p. 119]

Consider what you have in the smallest chosen library. A company of the wisest and wittiest men that could be picked out of all civil countries, in a thousand years, have set in best order the results of their learning and wisdom. The men themselves were hid and inaccessible, solitary, impatient of interruption, fenced by etiquette; but the thought which they did not uncover to their bosom friend is here written out in transparent words to us, the strangers of another age.

RALPH WALDO EMERSON, "Books,"
Society and Solitude (1870)

He that revels in a well‹chosen library, has innumerable dishes, and all of admirable flavour.

WILLIAM GODWIN, "Early Taste for Reading," *The Enquirer* (1797)

Libraries are reservoirs of strength, grace and wit, reminders of order, calm and continuity, lakes of mental energy, neither warm nor cold, light nor dark. The pleasure they give is steady, unorgastic, reliable, deep and long‹lasting. In any library in the world, I am at home, unselfconscious, still and absorbed.

GERMAINE GREER, *Daddy, We Hardly Knew You* (1989)

I no sooner come into the Library, but I bolt the door to me, excluding lust, ambition, avarice, and all such vices, whose nurse is idleness, the mother of ignorance, and Melancholy herself, and in the very lap of eternity, amongst so many divine souls, I take my seat, with so lofty a spirit and sweet content, that I pity all our great ones, and rich men that know not this happiness.

HEINSIUS, keeper of the library in Leyden, Holland, in *The Anatomy of Melancholy* by Robert Burton (1621)

One of [the lamasery's] features . . . was a very delightful library, lofty and spacious, and containing a multitude of books so retiringly housed in bays and alcoves that the whole atmosphere was more of wisdom than of learning, of good manners rather than seriousness.

JAMES HILTON, *Lost Horizon* (1933)

Every library should try to be complete on something, if it were only on the history of pin-heads.

OLIVER WENDELL HOLMES, SR., *The Poet at the Breakfast-Table* (1872)

If we had a good library, we should be in the situation of the Turks with their seraglios, which are a great improvement upon our petty exclusivenesses.

LEIGH HUNT, *Wedded to Books* (c. 1850) [See Ralph Waldo Emerson, p. 117]

Bring your questions to any good library, and most likely you will match them up with answers. Bring loneliness, and in books you will find the solace and company of other lives. Bring the gray of the everyday and you will lose it in the infinite colors of books. The great houses and protectors of books, libraries offer as many thousands of worlds as there are volumes on their shelves.

BEN JACOBS AND HELENA HJALMARSSON,
The Quotable Book Lover (1999)

If I were not a King, I would be an university man; and if it were so that I must be a prisoner, if I might have my wish, I would desire to have no other prison than that Library, and to be chained together with so many good authors.

KING JAMES I, on the Bodleian Library at Oxford,
in *The Anatomy of Melancholy* by Robert Burton (1621)

No place affords a more striking conviction of the vanity of human hopes than a public library.

DR. SAMUEL JOHNSON, in *The Rambler*, March 23, 1751

[**L**ibraries will someday] take the place of the dispensary . . . instead of giving us prescriptions of nauseous drugs, the physician will write down the titles of delightful books—books tonic or narcotic, stimulating or sedative, as our need may be.

RICHARD LE GALLIENNE, "Books as Doctors," *Attitudes and Avowals* (1910) [See William Drummond, p. 117]

The opening of a free, public library . . . is a most important event in the history of any town.

JAMES RUSSELL LOWELL, "Books and Libraries,"
Democracy and Other Addresses (1887)

Books are becoming everything to me. If I had at this moment any choice of life, I would bury myself in one of those immense libraries . . . and never pass a waking hour without a book before me.

THOMAS B. MACAULAY, *The Life and Letters of Thomas B. Macaulay,* edited by George Otto Trevelyan (1876)

What is more important in a library than anything else—than everything else—is the fact that it exists.

ARCHIBALD MACLEISH, "The Premise of Meaning,"
The American Scholar, June 5, 1972

The library wasn't simply where one had to go to get the books, it was a kind of exacting haven to which a city youngster willingly went for his lesson in restraint, and his training in self-control.

PHILIP ROTH, "The Newark Public Library,"
Reading Myself and Others (1975)

Libraries

The library is the temple of learning, and learning has liberated more people than all the ways in history.

CARL ROWAN, *American Libraries*

Come, and take choice of all my library,
And so beguile thy sorrow.

WILLIAM SHAKESPEARE, *Titus Andronicus* (1590)

My library
Was dukedom large enough.

WILLIAM SHAKESPEARE, *The Tempest* (1611)

I go into my library, and all history rolls before me. I breathe the morning air of the world while the scent of Eden's roses yet lingered in it, while it vibrated only to the world's first brood of nightingales, and to the laugh of Eve. I see the pyramids building; I hear the shoutings of the armies of Alexander; I feel the ground shake beneath the march of Cambyses, I sit as in a theatre—the stage is time, the play is the play of the world.

ALEXANDER SMITH, "Books and Garden," *Dreamthorp* (1863)

It seems to me one cannot sit down in that place without a heart full of grateful reverence. I own to have said my grace at the table, and to have thanked Heaven for this my English birthright, freely to partake of these beautiful books, and speak the truth I find there.

WILLIAM MAKEPEACE THACKERAY, on the Round Reading Room at the British Museum in London, in "The Round Room Comes to an End" by Angeline Goreau, *The New York Times Book Review*, November 9, 1997

No one will write books once they reach heaven, but there is an excellent library, containing all the books written up to date, including all the lost books and the ones that the authors burned when they came back from the last publisher.

EVELYN WAUGH, *Daily Chronicle*, March 18, 1930

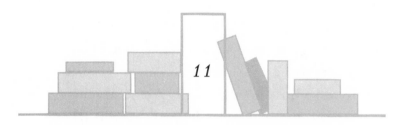

11

Good Books and Bad

CONFRONTED WITH THE enormous number of books that have already been published, and the many more that are published every year, we can sympathize with James M. Barrie's remark that "the printing-press is either the greatest blessing or the greatest curse of modern times, one sometimes forgets which."

Books being in at least one respect no different from anything else, it is unfortunately true that of all those millions of titles, some will be excellent, some will be truly bad, and the great majority will be mediocre. "There are always," as Peter S. Prescott says, "more books to condemn than to praise." The problem, of course, is in determining which is which. Regrettably, as Thomas De Quincey wrote, "One of the misfortunes of life is that one must read thousands of books only to discover that one need not have read them."

Of course, what is good and what is bad in books, as in all things, is largely subjective. This has not, however, deterred people from offering suggestions on how to make this important distinction, and some of the more trenchant are included in the pages that follow.

———

A good book is fruitful of other books; it perpetuates its fame from age to age, and makes eras in the lives of its readers.

A. BRONSON ALCOTT, *Tablets* (1868)

Good books, like good friends, are few and chosen; the more select the more enjoyable.

A. BRONSON ALCOTT, *Concord Days* (1872)

That is a good book which is opened with expectation, and closed with profit.

A. BRONSON ALCOTT, *Table-Talk* (1877)

Some books are undeservedly forgotten; none are undeservedly remembered.

W. H. AUDEN, "Reading," *The Dyer's Hand* (1962)

The reason why so few good books are written is that so few people who can write know anything.

WALTER BAGEHOT, "Shakespeare," *Literary Studies* (1879)

[**A** classic is] a book everyone is assumed to have read and often thinks they have.

ALAN BENNETT, "Independent on Sunday," January 27, 1991 [See Calvino, p. 128; Chesterton, p. 129; Kazin, p. 133; Miller, p. 134; Pound, p. 136; Van Doren, p. 137; and Winchester, p. 138]

All dull books are bad, and all tiresome books are either bad or maladroit or both.

ARNOLD BENNETT, *Things That Have Interested Me* (1926)

The test of a first-rate work, and a test of your sincerity in calling it a first-rate work, is that you finish it.

ARNOLD BENNETT, *Things That Have Interested Me* (1926)

The covers of this book are too far apart.

AMBROSE BIERCE, a one-sentence book review quoted in *Bitter Bierce* by C. H. Grattan (1929) [See Christopher Lehmann-Haupt, p. 133]

If those only wrote, who were sure of being read, we should have fewer authors; and the shelves of libraries would not groan beneath the weight of dusty tomes more voluminous than luminous.

LADY MARGUERITE BLESSINGTON, *The Confessions of an Elderly Lady* (1838)

A classic is a book that has never finished saying what it has to say.

ITALO CALVINO, *The Literature Machine* (1986) [See Bennett, p. 127; Chesterton, p. 129; Kazin, p. 133; Miller, p. 134; Pound, p. 136; Van Doren p. 137; and Winchester, p. 138]

There is no book so bad . . . but something good may be found in it.

MIGUEL DE CERVANTES SAAVEDRA, *Don Quixote* (1615)

Most of today's books have an air of having been written in one day from books read the night before.

SÉBASTIAN⋅ROCH⋅NICOLAS CHAMFORT, *Maxims and Thoughts* (1796)

A great classic means a man whom one can praise without having read.

G. K. CHESTERTON, "Tom Jones and Morality,"
All Things Considered (1908) [See Bennett, p. 127; Calvino,
p. 128; Kazin, p. 133; Miller, p. 134; Pound, p. 136; Van Doren,
p. 137; and Winchester, p. 138]

Let no book perish, unless it be such an one as it is your duty to throw into the fire. There is no such thing as a worthless book, though there are some far worse than worthless; no book which is not worth preserving, if its existence may be tolerated; as there are some men whom it may be proper to hang, but none who should be suffered to starve.

HARTLEY COLERIDGE, *Biographia Borealis* (1836)

I have but one book, but it is the best.

WILLIAM COLLINS, referring to the New Testament,
in *The Lives of the Most Eminent Poets* by Dr. Samuel
Johnson (1781)

Contemporary books do not keep. The quality in them which makes for their success is the first to go; they turn overnight.

CYRIL CONNOLLY, *Enemies of Promise* (1938)

Literature is the art of writing something that will be read twice.

CYRIL CONNOLLY, *Enemies of Promise* (1938)

[It is only in prison that] the acid test of what is readable can be found.

SIR EDWARD COOK, *More Literary Recreations* (1919)

One of the misfortunes of life is that one must read thousands of books only to discover that one need not have read them.

THOMAS DE QUINCEY

If I read a book and it makes my whole body so cold no fire can ever warm me, I know that is poetry. If I feel physically as if the top of my head were taken off, I know that is poetry. These are the only ways I know it. Is there any other way?

EMILY DICKINSON, *The Life and Letters of Emily Dickinson*, edited by Martha Gilbert Dickinson Bianchi (1924)

'Tis the good reader that makes the good book; . . . in every book he finds passages which seem confidences or asides hidden from all else and unmistakably meant for his ear.

RALPH WALDO EMERSON, "Success," *Society and Solitude* (1870)

People do not deserve to have good writing, they are so pleased with bad.

RALPH WALDO EMERSON, 1841, *Journals* (1909–1914)

Only two classes of books are of universal appeal: the very best and the very worst.

FORD MADOX FORD, *Joseph Conrad* (1924)

One always tends to overpraise a long book, because one has got through it.

E. M. FORSTER, "T. E. Lawrence," *Abinger Harvest: A Miscellany* (1927)

Even bad books are books, and therefore sacred.

GÜNTER GRASS, *The Tin Drum* (1959)

Some books are read in the parlour and some in the kitchen, but the test of a real genuine book is that it is read in both.

THOMAS CHANDLER HALIBURTON, *Wise Saws* (1855)

All good books are alike in that they are truer than if they had really happened, and after you are finished reading one you will feel that all that happened to you and afterwards it all belongs to you.

ERNEST HEMINGWAY, "Old Newsman Writes: A Letter from Cuba," *Esquire,* December 1934

All modern American literature comes from one book by Mark Twain called *Huckleberry Finn.* . . . American writing comes from that. There was nothing before. There has been nothing as good since.

ERNEST HEMINGWAY, *Green Hills of Africa* (1935)

The praise of ancient authors proceeds not from the reverence of the dead, but from the competition and mutual envy of the living.

THOMAS HOBBES, *Leviathan* (1651)

A bad book is as much of a labour to write as a good one; it comes as sincerely from the author's soul.

ALDOUS HUXLEY, *Point Counter Point* (1928)

Books worth reading are worth re-reading.

HOLBROOK JACKSON, *Maxims of Books and Reading* (1934)

A classic is a book that survives the circumstances that made it possible yet alone keeps those circumstances alive.

ALFRED KAZIN, in *The New Republic,* August 29, 1988 [See Bennett, p. 127; Calvino, p. 128; Chesterton, p. 129; Miller, p. 134; Pound, p. 136; Van Doren, p. 137; and Winchester, p. 138]

If you find the Miltons in certain parts dirtied and soiled with a crumb of right Gloucester blacked in the candle (my usual supper), or peradventure a stray ash of tobacco wafted into the crevices, look to that passage more especially: depend upon it: it contains good matter.

CHARLES LAMB, in a letter to Samuel Taylor Coleridge, *The Letters of Charles Lamb,* edited by E. V. Lucas (1935)

The only trouble with this book is that its covers are too close together.

CHRISTOPHER LEHMANN∗HAUPT, on *With Charity Toward None* by Florence King, in *The New York Times,* April 9, 1992 [See Ambrose Bierce, p. 127]

I read [D. H. Lawrence's *Lady Chatterley's Lover*] and I don't think I would object to my wife reading it—nor would I object to my daughter reading it. Of course, I am not so sure I would want my gamekeeper to read it.

MEMBER OF PARLIAMENT, in *Sing Out!* magazine, October–November 1962

In the main, there are two sorts of books: those that no one reads and those that no one ought to read.

H. L. MENCKEN, *A Little Book in C Major* (1916)

Every man with a belly full of the classics is an enemy of the human race.

HENRY MILLER, *Tropic of Cancer* (1939) [See Bennett, p. 127; Calvino, p. 128; Chesterton, p. 129; Kazin, p. 133; Pound, p. 136; Van Doren, p. 137; and Winchester, p. 138]

I have only read one book in my life, and that is *White Fang*. It's so frightfully good that I've never bothered to read another.

NANCY MITFORD

Everywhere I go I'm asked if I think the university stifles writers. My opinion is that they don't stifle enough of them. There's many a best-seller that could have been prevented by a good teacher.

FLANNERY O'CONNOR

A book that furnishes no quotations is . . . no book—
it is a plaything.

THOMAS LOVE PEACOCK, *Crotchet Castle* (1831)

We are becoming boisterous and arrogant in the pride
of a too speedily assumed literary freedom. . . . So far
from being ashamed of the many disgraceful literary
failures to which our own inordinate vanities
and misapplied patriotism have lately given birth, and
so far from deeply lamenting that these daily puerilities
are of home manufacture, we adhere pertinaciously
to our original blindly conceived idea, and thus often
find ourselves involved in the gross paradox of liking
a stupid book the better, because, sure enough, its
stupidity is American.

EDGAR ALLAN POE, "Review of Poems by Drake and
Halleck," *Southern Literary Messenger*, April 1836

The enormous multiplication of books in every branch
of knowledge is one of the greatest evils of this age;
since it presents one of the most serious obstacles to the
acquisition of correct information, by throwing in the
reader's way piles of lumber in which he must painfully
grope for the scraps of useful matter, peradventure
interspersed.

EDGAR ALLAN POE, *Marginalia* (1844–1849)

A classic is classic not because it conforms to certain structural rules, or fits certain definitions (of which its author had quite probably never heard). It is classic because of a certain eternal and irrepressible freshness.

EZRA POUND, *The ABC of Reading* (1934) [See Bennett, p. 127; Calvino, p. 128; Chesterton, p. 129; Kazin, p. 133; Miller, p. 134; Van Doren, p. 137; and Winchester, p. 138]

There are always more books to condemn than to praise.

PETER S. PRESCOTT, *Soundings* (1972)

There exists one book, which, to my taste, furnishes the happiest treatise of natural education. What then is this marvelous book? Is it Aristotle? Is it Pliny, is it Buffon? No—it is *Robinson Crusoe*.

JEAN-JACQUES ROUSSEAU, *Emile; or, Treatise on Education* (1762)

You can never read bad literature too little, nor good literature too much.

ARTHUR SCHOPENHAUER, "On Books and Reading," *The Art of Literature* (1818)

Read Homer once, and you can read no more;
For all books else appear so mean, so poor,
Verse will seem prose; but still persist to read,
And Homer will be all the books you need.

JOHN SHEFFIELD, *Essay on Poetry* (1682)

The good book is always a book of travel; it is about a life's journey.

H. M. TOMLINSON

A classic is a book that doesn't have to be written again.

CARL VAN DOREN [See Bennett, p. 127; Calvino, p. 128; Chesterton, p. 129; Kazin, p. 133; Miller, p. 134; Pound, p. 136; and Winchester, p. 138]

There is no such thing as a moral or an immoral book. Books are well written, or badly written. That is all.

OSCAR WILDE, *The Picture of Dorian Gray* (1891)

Good Books and Bad

A classic is something that everybody wants to have read and nobody wants to read.

CALEB T. WINCHESTER, a professor at Wesleyan University, quoted by Mark Twain in "The Disappearance of Literature," a speech given on November 20, 1900 [See Bennett, p. 127; Calvino, p. 128; Chesterton, p. 129; Kazin, p. 133; Miller, p. 134; Pound, p. 136; and Van Doren, p. 137]

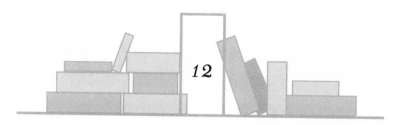

12

The Comfort Found in Books

OF ALL THE BENEFITS that can be derived from
books and reading, one that seems to be cited more
often than almost any other is that of the comfort
books provide. Perhaps not surprisingly, these comments
are frequently couched in terms of friendship, such as
A. Bronson Alcott referring to books as "the most
mannerly of companions." Perhaps somewhat more
surprisingly, though, books are also often compared to
medicine. Note, for example, Arthur James Balfour
declaring "There is no mood to which a man may not
administer the appropriate medicine at the cost of
reaching down a volume from his bookshelf."

Even more often, though, books and reading are
presented as a refuge from the world, a safe haven where

nothing and no one can intrude, a "fair land," as Arthur Conan Doyle calls them, "whither worry and vexation can follow you no more." And there is little surprise that those who consider the world a difficult place to endure perceive books as such, for they can, as Henry Cabot Lodge wrote, provide a "blessed forgetfulness of the din and sorrows that surround us. Here, for the asking, the greatest geniuses will speak to us and we can rise into a purer atmosphere and become close neighbors to the stars."

There are times when I think that the ideal library is composed solely of reference books. They are like understanding friends—always ready to meet your mood, always ready to change the subject when you have had enough of this or that.

J. DONALD ADAMS, *The New York Times*, April 1, 1956

Books are the most mannerly of companions, accessible at all times, in all moods, frankly declaring the author's mind, without offence.

A. BRONSON ALCOTT, *Concord Days* (1872)

[Books contain] many a powerful opiate to soothe us into a sweet and temporary forgetfulness.

ANONYMOUS, "Book-Lore," *Fraser's Magazine,* 1847

It were too long to go over the particular remedies which [book] learning doth minister to all the diseases of the mind; sometimes purging the ill humours, sometimes opening the obstructions, sometimes healing the wounds and exulcerations thereof, and the like.

FRANCIS BACON, "Of the Advancement of Learning," *Essays* (1625)

There is no mood to which a man may not administer the appropriate medicine at the cost of reaching down a volume from his bookshelf.

LORD ARTHUR JAMES BALFOUR, *Essays and Addresses* (1893)

He that loveth a book will never want a faithful friend, a wholesome counsellor, a cheerful companion, an effectual comforter.

ISAAC BARROW, "Of Industry in Our Particular Calling as Scholars," *The Works* (1683)

Literature was meant to give pleasure, to excite interest, to banish solitude, to make the fireside more attractive than the tavern, to give joy to those who are still capable of joy, and—why should we not admit it?—to drug sorrow and divert thought.

AUGUSTINE BIRRELL, Introduction to *The Life of Samuel Johnson* by James Boswell (1896)

Who is he that is now wholly overcome with idleness, or otherwise involved in a labyrinth of worldly cares, troubles, and discontents, that will not be much lightened in his mind by reading of some enticing story, true or feigned, where (as in a glass) he shall observe what our forefathers have done, the beginnings, ruins, falls, periods of Commonwealths, private men's actions displayed to the life, etc.

ROBERT BURTON, *The Anatomy of Melancholy* (1621)

[Books] nourish youth; delight old age; adorn prosperity; afford a refuge and solace in adversity; forming our delights at home; anything but hindrances abroad; they are our nightly associates; our indoor and out-of-door companions.

CICERO, *Pro Archia*

Books are a guide in youth, and an entertainment for age. They support us under solitude, and keep us from becoming a burden to ourselves. They help us forget the crossness of men and things, compose our cares and our passions, and lay our disappointments to sleep. When we are weary of living, we may repair to the dead, who have nothing of peevishness, pride, or design in their conversation.

JEREMY COLLIER, "Of the Entertainment of Books," *Essays upon Several Moral Subjects* (1698)

The library of a good man is one of his most constant, cheerful, and instructive companions; and as it has delighted him in youth, so will it solace him in old age.

THOMAS FROGNALL DIBDIN, *The Bibliomania or Book Madness* (1809)

He ate and drank the precious words,
His spirits grew robust;
He knew no more that he was poor,
Nor that his frame was dust.
He danced along the dingy days,
And this bequest of wings
Was but a book. What liberty
A loosened spirit brings!

EMILY DICKINSON, "A Book (1)," *Poems* (1890)

I care not how humble your bookshelf may be, nor how lowly the room which it adorns. Close the door of that room behind you, shut off with it all the cares of the outer world, plunge back into the soothing company of the great dead, and then you are through the magic portal into that fair land whither worry and vexation can follow you no more.

ARTHUR CONAN DOYLE, *Through the Magic Door* (1907)

In the highest civilization the book is still the highest delight. He who has once known its satisfactions is provided with a resource against calamity. Angels they are to us of entertainment, sympathy, and provocation— silent guides, tractable prophets, historians, and singers, whose embalmed life is the highest feat of art; who now cast their moonlight illumination over solitude, weariness, and fallen fortunes.

RALPH WALDO EMERSON, "Quotation and Originality," *Letters and Social Aims* (1876)

Books cannot change. A thousand years hence they are what you find them today, speaking the same words, holding forth the same comfort.

EUGENE FIELD, *Love Affairs of a Bibliomaniac* (1896)

When our house is in mourning, we turn to . . . the great books written by those who have walked through the Valley of the Shadow, yet have come out sweet and wholesome, with words of wisdom and counsel for the afflicted. One book through which beats the great heart of a man who has suffered yet grew strong under the lash of fate is worth more than a thousand books that teach no real lesson of life, that are as broken cisterns holding no water, when the soul is athirst and cries out for refreshment.

GEORGE HAMLIN FITCH, *Comfort Found in Good Old Books* (1911)

To divert at any time a troublesome fancy, run to thy books; they always receive thee with the same kindness.

THOMAS FULLER, "Of Books," *The Holy State and the Profane State* (1642)

It is life that shakes and rocks us; it is literature which stabilizes and confirms.

HEATHCOTE WILLIAM GARROD, *The Profession of Poetry and Other Lectures* (1929)

To what end do I read and remember? Surely, as foolish a question as ever man put to himself. You read for your own pleasure, for your solace and strengthening. Pleasure, then, purely selfish? Solace which endures for an hour and strengthening for no combat? Ay, but I know, I know. With what heart should I live here in my cottage, waiting for life's end, were it not for those hours of seeming idle reading?

GEORGE GISSING, *The Private Papers of Henry Ryecroft* (1903)

I armed her against the censure of the world, showed her that books were sweet unreproaching companions to the miserable, and that if they could not bring us to enjoy life, they would at least teach us to endure it.

OLIVER GOLDSMITH, *The Vicar of Wakefield* (1766)

If fortune turns her face once more in kindness upon me before I go, I may chance, some quiet day, to lay my overbeating temples on a book, and so have the death I envy most.

LEIGH HUNT, *My Books* (1823)

Let your bookcases and your shelves be your gardens and your pleasure-grounds. Pluck the fruit that grows therein, gather the roses, the spices, and the myrrh. If your soul be satiate and weary, change from garden to garden, from furrow to furrow, from sight to sight. Then will your desire renew itself and your soul be satisfied with delight.

JUDAH IBN TIBBON, in *Jewish Life in the Middle Ages* by Israel Abrahams (1896)

The scholar only knows how dear these silent, yet eloquent, companions of pure thoughts and innocent hours become in the season of adversity. When all that is worldly turns to dross around us, these only retain their steady value. When friends grow cold, and the converse of intimates languishes into vapid civility and commonplace, these only continue the unaltered countenance of happier days, and cheer us with that true friendship which never deceived hope nor deserted sorrow.

WASHINGTON IRVING, *The Sketch Book of Geoffrey Crayon, Gent.* (1819–1820)

If I were in the country, and were distressed with the malady [of melancholy], I would force myself to take a book; and every time I did it I should find it the easier.

DR. SAMUEL JOHNSON, in *The Life of Samuel Johnson* by James Boswell (1791)

Literature is my Utopia. Here I am not disenfranchised. No barrier of the senses shuts me out from the sweet, gracious discourse of my book friends. They talk to me without embarrassment or awkwardness.

HELEN KELLER, *The Story of My Life* (1902)

I have sought rest everywhere, and only found it in corners and books.

THOMAS À KEMPIS, *Imitation of Christ* (1471) [See Robert Southey, p. 150]

Here among the books we can pass out of this work-a-day world, never more tormented, more in anguish than now, and find, for a brief hour at least, happiness, perchance consolation, certainly another world and a blessed forgetfulness of the din and sorrows that surround us. Here, for the asking, the greatest geniuses will speak to us and we can rise into a purer atmosphere and become close neighbors to the stars.

HENRY CABOT LODGE

The love of learning, the sequestered nooks,
And all the sweet serenity of books.

HENRY WADSWORTH LONGFELLOW, *Morituri Salutamus* (1875)

What a sense of security in an old book which Time has criticized for us!

JAMES RUSSELL LOWELL, "A Library of Old Authors," *My Study Windows* (1871)

To divert me from any importunate imagination or insinuating conceit, there is no better way than to have recourse unto books; with ease they allure me to them, and with facility they remove them all.

MICHEL EYQUEM DE MONTAIGNE, "Of Three Commerces or Societies," *Essays* (1580)

I have never known any distress that an hour's reading did not relieve.

CHARLES DE SECONDAT, BARON DE LA BRÈDE ET DE MONTESQUIEU, *Pensées Diverses* (1899)

Just the knowledge that a good book is awaiting one at the end of a long day makes that day happier.

KATHLEEN NORRIS

Books are the blessed chloroform of the mind.

JAMES PAYN, "What English Literature Gives Us," *Chambers's Journal* (1864)

Literature is both my job and my comfort: it can add to every happiness and there is no sorrow it cannot console.

PLINY THE YOUNGER, *Letters*

Muddling among old books has the quality of a sedative, and saves the tear and wear of an overwrought brain.

SIR WALTER SCOTT, *Journal* (1890)

I too have found repose where he [Thomas à Kempis] did, in books and retirement, but it was there alone I sought it; to these my nature, under the direction of a merciful Providence, led me betimes, and the world can offer nothing which should tempt me from them.

ROBERT SOUTHEY, *Sir Thomas More: or, Colloquies on the Progress and Prospects of Society* (1829) [See Thomas à Kempis, p. 148]

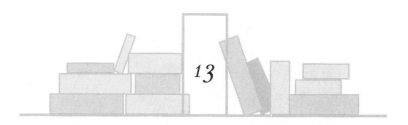

13

Lending and Borrowing Books

"OUR BOOKS," SAYS Roger Rosenblatt, "are ourselves, our characters, our insulation against those very people who would take away our books." No wonder the question of lending and borrowing books is such a volatile one for book lovers.

Anatole Broyard once wrote that he felt about lending books the way "most fathers feel about their daughters living out of wedlock." Although times have changed some and the simile may no longer be as appropriate as it once was, the idea remains the same: we are reluctant—to say the least—to lend our books to anyone.

On the other hand, many of us have no such compunction about borrowing books and are more than willing to take advantage of our friends' libraries, and their foolhardy willingness to lend us books. We call such friends foolhardy because, once we have a book in our possession, regardless of whose book it is, we are not inclined to part with it, even to return it to its original owner. As Anatole France wisely counsels, "Never lend books—nobody ever returns them; the only books I have in my library are those which people have lent me."

———————

Ior him that stealeth, or borroweth and returneth not, this book from its owner, let it change into a serpent in his hand and rend him. Let him be struck with palsy, and all his members blasted. Let him languish in pain crying aloud for mercy, and let there be no surcease to this agony till he sing in dissolution. Let bookworms gnaw his entrails . . . and when at last he goeth to his final punishment, let the flames of Hell consume him forever.

ANONYMOUS "curse" on book thieves from the monastery of San Pedro, Barcelona

The book borrower . . . proves himself to be an inveterate collector of books not so much by the fervor with which he guards his borrowed treasures . . . as by his failure to read these books.

WALTER BENJAMIN, "Unpacking My Library,"
Illuminations (1955)

Great collections of books are subject to certain accidents besides the damp, the worms, and the rats; one not less common is that of the borrowers, not to say a word of the purloiners.

ISAAC D'ISRAELI, "The Bibliomania," *Curiosities of Literature* (1791–1834)

A book-collector whose books belonged also to his friends, even indirectly, even in a purely sentimental fashion, could not be a book-collector for a longer time than a week.

H. P. DU BOIS, *Four Private Libraries of New York* (1892)

Never lend books—nobody ever returns them; the only books I have in my library are those which people have lent me.

ANATOLE FRANCE, *La Vie Littéraire* (1888–1892)
[See Frank Hird, below]

I cannot comfortably read a book belonging to another person because I feel all the time afraid of spoiling it.

LAFCADIO HEARN, in *The Life and Letters of Lafcadio Hearn* by Elizabeth Bisland (1906)

The owner of a country house was showing some visitors over a superb library. "Do you ever lend books?" he was asked. "No," he replied promptly, "only fools lend books." Then, waving his hand to a many-shelved section filled with handsomely bound volumes, he added, "All those books once belonged to fools."

FRANK HIRD, in the *Times,* March 7, 1928 [See Anatole France, above]

Everything comes t' him who waits but a loaned book.

KIN HUBBARD, *Abe Martin's Primer* (1914)

A friend thinks no more of borrowing a book nowadays, than a Roman did of borrowing a man's wife; and what is worse, we are so far gone in our immoral notions on this subject, that we even lend it as easily as Cato did his spouse.

LEIGH HUNT, *Wedded to Books* (c. 1850)

I own I borrow books with as much facility as I lend. I cannot see a work that interests me on another person's shelf, without a wish to carry it off: but, I repeat, that I have been much more sinned against than sinning in the article of non-return; and am scrupulous in the article of intention.

LEIGH HUNT, *My Books* (1823)

The good bookman at his best will prefer, except in an emergency, to possess rather than borrow books, for a book is not fully known unless it is owned as well as read.

HOLBROOK JACKSON, *The Anatomy of Bibliomania* (1930)

Of those who borrow some read slow; some mean to read and don't read; and some neither read nor mean to read, but borrow to leave you an opinion of their sagacity.

CHARLES LAMB, *The Letters of Charles Lamb*, edited by E. V. Lucas (1935)

Your *borrowers* of books—those mutilators of collections, spoilers of the symmetry of shelves, and creators of odd volumes.

CHARLES LAMB, "The Two Races of Men," *Essays of Elia* (1823)

Reader, if haply thou art blessed with a moderate collection, be shy of showing it; or if thy heart overfloweth to lend them, lend thy books; but let it be to such a one as . . . will return them . . . with usury; enriched with annotations, tripling their value. . . . I counsel thee, shut not thy heart, nor thy library.

CHARLES LAMB, "The Two Races of Men," *Essays of Elia* (1823)

On the Return of a Book Lent to a Friend

I give hearty and humble thanks for the safe return
of this book, which having endured the perils of my
friend's bookcase and the bookcases of my friend's
friends, now returns to me in reasonably good condition.
I give hearty and humble thanks that my friend did not
see fit to give this book to his infant for a plaything,
nor use it as an ash tray for his burning cigar, nor as a
teething-ring for his mastiff. When I loaned this book,
I deemed it as lost; I was resigned to the business of
the long parting; I never thought to look upon its pages
again. But now that my book has come back to me,
I rejoice and am exceedingly glad! Bring hither the
fatted morocco and let us rebind the volume and set it
on the shelf of honor, for this my book was lent and is
returned again. Presently, therefore, I may return some
of the books I myself have borrowed.

CHRISTOPHER MORLEY, *The Haunted Bookshop* (1919)

Charles Lamb was right when he called book borrowers
"mutilators of collections, spoilers of the symmetry of
shelves, and creators of odd volumes." The interesting
thing about the feeling of loss when a book is borrowed
is that the book's quality rarely matters. So mysterious is
the power of books in our lives that every loss is a serious

loss, every hole in the shelf a crater. Our books are ourselves, our characters, our insulation against those very people who would take away our books.

ROGER ROSENBLATT, in *At Home with Books* by Estelle Ellis, Caroline Seebohm, and Christopher Simon Sykes (1995)

For some reason a book borrower feels that a book, once taken, is his own. This removes both memory and guilt from the transaction. Making matters worse, the lender believes it, too. To keep up appearances, he may solemnly extract an oath that the book be brought back as soon as possible; the borrower answering with matching solemnity that the Lord might seize his eyes were he to do otherwise. But it is all play. Once gone, the book is gone forever. The lender, fearing rudeness, never asks for it again. The borrower never stoops to raise the subject.

ROGER ROSENBLATT, *Bibliomania,* a one-man show first performed at New York's American Place Theater in 1994

There's no spectacle that is as terrifying as the sight of a guest in your house whom you catch staring at your books. It is not the judgmental possibility that is frightening. The fact that one's sense of discrimination is exposed by his books. Indeed, most people would much prefer to see the guest first scan, then peer and turn away in boredom or disapproval. Alas, too often the eyes, dark with calculation, shift from title to title as from floozie to floozie in an overheated dance hall. Nor is that the worst. It is when those eyes stop moving that the heart, too, stops. The guest's body twitches; his hand floats up to where his eyes have led it. There is nothing to be done. You freeze. He smiles. You hear the question even as it forms: "Would you mind if I borrowed this book?"

ROGER ROSENBLATT, *Bibliomania,* a one‑man show first performed at New York's American Place Theater in 1994

Please return this book; I find that though many of my friends are poor arithmeticians, they are nearly all good book‑keepers.

SIR WALTER SCOTT, an inscription in one of his books

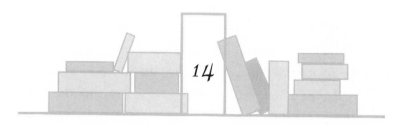

Books and the Young

AS ADULTS, MOST OF US take for granted not only the pleasure we take in reading but even our very ability to read. It seems to be so natural an activity that we don't even think about it. And yet, deciphering those little marks on paper, learning to recognize them as letters, then forming them into words, and finally meanings, isn't really natural at all. Nor, in fact, is it easy. Nevertheless, we all manage to do it, and it's often an extraordinary experience.

Although not all of us can recall that experience, there seem to be many who do. "I remember," wrote Graham Greene in *The Lost Childhood*, "the suddenness with which a key turned in a lock, and I found I could read—not just sentences . . . but a real book. Now the future stood around on bookshelves everywhere." Clearly, for Greene, as for many others, the experience is an epiphany they never forget.

At the same time, however, while learning to read has the beneficial effect of opening the world to us, it might also be likened to Adam and Eve's tasting the forbidden fruit of the tree of knowledge. For, as Neil Postman has written, "Reading is the scourge of childhood because, in a sense, it creates adulthood."

You may perhaps be brought to acknowledge that it is very well worthwhile to be tormented for two or three years of one's life, for the sake of being able to read all the rest of it.

JANE AUSTEN, *Northanger Abbey* (1818)

No man has a right to bring up his children without surrounding them with books, if he has the means to buy them. It is a wrong to his family. He cheats them! Children learn to read by being in the presence of books. The love of knowledge comes with reading and grows upon it. And the love of knowledge, in a young mind, is almost a warrant against the inferior excitement of passions and vices.

HENRY WARD BEECHER, *The Sermons of Henry Ward Beecher* (1870)

Child! Do not throw this book about;
Refrain from the unholy pleasure
Of cutting all the pictures out!
Preserve it as your chiefest treasure.

HILAIRE BELLOC, *A Bad Child's Book of Beasts* (1896)

I remember . . . the suddenness with which a key turned
in a lock, and I found I could read—not just sentences . . .
but a real book. Now the future stood around on
bookshelves everywhere.

GRAHAM GREENE, *The Lost Childhood* (1951)

From your parents you learn love and laughter and
how to put one foot before the other. But when books
are opened you discover that you have wings.

HELEN HAYES, *On Reflection* (1968)

Read [books] as you grow up with all the satisfaction in
your power, and make much of them. It is, perhaps, the
greatest pleasure you will have in life; the one you will
think of longest, and repent of least. If my life had been
more full of calamity than it has been (much more than I
hope yours will be), I would live it over again, my poor
little boy, to have read the books I did in my youth.

WILLIAM HAZLITT, *On the Conduct of Life; or Advice to
a Schoolboy* (c. 1820)

Education begins by teaching children to read and ends by making most of them hate reading.

HOLBROOK JACKSON, *Maxims of Books and Reading* (1934)

I am always for getting a boy forward in his learning; for that is a sure good. I would let him at first read any English book which happens to engage his attention; because you have done a great deal when you have brought him to have entertainment from a book. He'll get better books afterward.

DR. SAMUEL JOHNSON, in *The Life of Samuel Johnson* by James Boswell (1791)

In my early years, I read very hard. It is a sad reflection, but a true one, that I knew almost as much at eighteen as I do now [at fifty-four]. My judgement, to be sure, was not so good; but I had all the facts. I remember very well, when I was at Oxford, an old gentleman said to me, "Young man, ply your book diligently now and acquire a stock of knowledge; for when years come upon you, you will find that poring upon books will be but an irksome task."

DR. SAMUEL JOHNSON, in *The Life of Samuel Johnson* by James Boswell (1791)

Whilst you stand deliberating which book your son shall read first, another boy has read both; read anything five hours a day, and you will soon be learned.

DR. SAMUEL JOHNSON, in "Books," *Society and Solitude* by Ralph Waldo Emerson (1870)

The memory of having been read to is a solace one carries through adulthood. It can wash over a multitude of parental sins.

KATHLEEN ROCKWELL LAWRENCE

Any kid who has two parents who are interested in him and has a house full of books isn't poor.

SAM LEVENSON, in *Readers Digest,* January 1, 1972

No book is really worth reading at the age of ten which is not equally (and often far more) worth reading at the age of fifty and beyond.

C. S. LEWIS

Reading is the scourge of childhood because, in a sense, it creates adulthood.

NEIL POSTMAN, "Where There Were No Children," *The Disappearance of Childhood* (1982)

No days, perhaps, of all our childhood are ever so fully lived as those that we had regarded as not being lived at all: days spent wholly with a favorite book.

MARCEL PROUST, introduction to *Sesame and Lilies* by John Ruskin (1906)

In most of our childhoods there have been those books beloved, not because they are marvelous children's books, but because they are marvelous books.

ANNA QUINDLEN, *The New York Times Book Review,* March 3, 1991

There may be no more pleasing picture in the world than that of a child peering into a book—the past and the future entrancing each other.

ROGER ROSENBLATT, "Would You Mind If I Borrowed This Book?" *The Man in the Water* (1994)

One of the greatest gifts adults can give—to their offspring and to their society—is to read to children.

CARL SAGAN, in *Parade,* March 6, 1994

Children don't read to find their identity, to free themselves from guilt, to quench the thirst for rebellion or to get rid of alienation. They have no use for psychology. They detest sociology. They still believe in God, the family, angels, devils, witches, goblins, logic, clarity, punctuation, and other such obsolete stuff. . . . When a book is boring, they yawn openly. They don't expect their writer to redeem humanity, but leave to adults such childish illusions.

ISAAC BASHEVIS SINGER

It had been startling and disappointing to me to find out that story books had been written by people, that books were not natural wonders, coming of themselves like grass.

EUDORA WELTY, *One Writer's Beginnings* (1984)

Books were my pass to personal freedom. I learned to read at age three, and soon discovered there was a whole world to conquer that went beyond our farm in Mississippi.

OPRAH WINFREY, in *A Little Learning Is a Dangerous Thing*, edited by James Charlton (1994)

Books and the Young

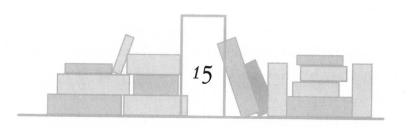

15

What Books Can~and Cannot~Teach Us

CERTAINLY NO THINKING PERSON has ever doubted that we can learn a great deal from books. Thomas Carlyle wrote, in 1841: "The true University of these days is a collection of books," and it is no less true today than it was in Victorian England or, for that matter, at any other time in recorded history.

On the other hand, as many here point out, there is much that cannot be learned from books, much that no one else can teach us and that can be gathered only from our own experience. Those who argue as much would no doubt urge us to take care to avoid being described, as Robert Browning does the subject of his poem "The Grammarian's Funeral," as a man who "decided not to Live but Know."

Equally—if not more—important are those who warn us not to confuse knowledge with wisdom. While the former, they acknowledge, can be gathered from books, the latter can only be acquired as a result of our own thought processes. Or, as Sébastian-Roch-Nicolas Chamfort put it more than two centuries ago, "What one knows best is . . . what one has learned not from books but as a result of books, through the reflections to which they have given rise."

A single conversation across the table with a wise man is better than ten years' study of books.

ANONYMOUS CHINESE SAYING [See Michel Eyquem de Montaigne, p. 178, and Woodrow Wilson, p. 182]

Knowledge without wisdom is a load of books on the back of an ass.

ANONYMOUS JAPANESE PROVERB

He had read much . . . but his contemplation was more than his reading. He was wont to say that if he had read

as much as other men, he should have known no more
than other men.

JOHN AUBREY, "Thomas Hobbes," *Brief Lives* (1690)

You will find something more in woods than in books.
Trees and stones will teach you that which you can never
learn from masters.

SAINT BERNARD, *Epistle 106*

More is got from one book on which the thought
settles for a definite end in knowledge, than from
libraries skimmed over by a wandering eye. A cottage
flower gives honey to the bee, a king's garden none to the
butterfly.

EDWARD BULWER⸱LYTTON, *Caxtoniana* (1863)

To read without reflecting, is like eating without digesting.

EDMUND BURKE

But the place where we are to get knowledge, even
theoretic knowledge, is the Books themselves! It depends
on what we read, after all manner of professors have

done their best for us. The true University of these days is a collection of books.

THOMAS CARLYLE, "The Hero as a Man of Letters," *On Heroes, Hero-Worship, and the Heroic* (1841)

There is nothing more injurious to the faculties than to keep poring over books continually without attempting to exhibit any of our own conceptions.

THOMAS CARLYLE, in a letter to Jane Welsh, April 30, 1822, *Early Letters of Thomas Carlyle,* edited by Charles Eliot Norton (1886)

What one knows best is . . . what one has learned not from books but as a result of books, through the reflections to which they have given rise.

SÉBASTIAN-ROCH-NICOLAS CHAMFORT, *Maxims and Thoughts* (1796)

As in the choice and reading of good books principally consists the enabling and advancement of a man's knowledge and learning; yet if it be not mixed with the conversation of discreet, able, and understanding men, they can make little use of their reading, either for themselves or the commonwealth where they live. There is not a more common proverb than this, That the Greatest Clerks be not always the wisest men.

GREY BRYDGES, LORD CHANDOS,
Horae Subsecivae (c. 1600)

All you learn and all you can read will be of little use if you do not think and reason upon it yourself. One reads to know other people's thoughts; but if we take them upon trust, without examining and comparing them with our own, it is really living upon other people's scraps or retailing other people's goods. To know the thoughts of others is of use because it suggests thoughts to oneself and helps one to form a judgment, but to repeat other people's thoughts without considering whether they are right or wrong is the talent only of a parrot or at most a player.

PHILIP DORMER STANHOPE, EARL OF
CHESTERFIELD, *Letters to His Son* (1774)

A man may as well expect to grow stronger by always eating, as wiser by always reading. Too much over-charges Nature, and turns more into disease than nourishment. 'Tis thought and digestion which makes books serviceable, and gives health and vigour to the Mind.

JEREMY COLLIER, "Of the Entertainment of Books,"
Essays upon Several Moral Subjects (1698)

If books are well chosen, they neither dull the Appetite, nor strain the Capacity . . . [but rather] they refresh the Inclination, and strengthen the Power, and improve under Experiment: and is best of all, they Entertain and Perfect at the same time, convey Wisdom and Knowledge through Pleasure.

JEREMY COLLIER, "Of the Entertainment of Books," *Essays upon Several Moral Subjects* (1698)

He that sets out on the journey of life, with a profound knowledge of books, but a shallow knowledge of men, with much sense of others, but little of his own, will find himself as completely at a loss on occasions of common and of constant recurrence, as a Dutchman without his pipe, a Frenchman without his mistress, an Italian without his fiddle, or an Englishman without his umbrella.

CHARLES CALEB COLTON, *Lacon: or, Many Things in Few Words; Addressed to Those Who Think* (1823)

But what strange art, what magic can dispose
The troubled mind to change its native woes?
Or lead us willing from ourselves, to see
Other more wretched, more undone than we?
This books can do—nor this alone: they give
New views to life, and teach us how to live;

They soothe the grieved, the stubborn they chastise;
Fools they admonish, and confirm the wise,
Their aid they yield to all: they never shun
The man of sorrow, nor the wretch undone;
Unlike the hard, the selfish, and the proud,
They fly not from the suppliant crowd;
Nor tell to various people various things,
But show to subjects, what they show to Kings.

GEORGE CRABBE, *The Library* (1781)

Books, we are told, propose to *instruct* or to *amuse*.
Indeed! The true antithesis to knowledge, in this case,
is not *pleasure*, but *power*. All that is literature seeks
to communicate power; all that is not literature, to
communicate knowledge.

THOMAS DE QUINCEY, "Letters to a Young Man Whose
Education Has Been Neglected," in *London Magazine*,
January–July 1823

Experience is the child of Thought, and Thought is
the child of action. We cannot learn men from books.

BENJAMIN DISRAELI, *Vivian Grey* (1826)

What can we see, read, acquire, but ourselves. Take the book, my friend, and read your eyes out, you will never find there what I find.

RALPH WALDO EMERSON, *Journals,* edited by Edward Waldo Emerson and Waldo Emerson Forbes (1914)

It is a vanity to persuade the world one hath learning, by getting a great library. As soon shall I believe every one is valiant that hath a well-furnished armoury.

THOMAS FULLER, "Of Books," *The Holy State and the Profane State* (1642)

Read not Books alone, but Man also; and chiefly thyself.

THOMAS FULLER, *Introductio ad Prudentiam* (1731)

Books give not wisdom where was none before,
But where some is, there reading makes it more.

SIR JOHN HARINGTON, *Epigrams* (1615)

The best service a book can render you is not to impart truth, but to make you think it out for yourself.

ELBERT HUBBARD, *The Note Book of Elbert Hubbard,* compiled by Elbert Hubbard II (1927)

$\mathfrak{I}$t is books that teach us to refine on our pleasures when young; and which, having taught us, enable us to recall them with satisfaction when old.

LEIGH HUNT

$\mathbf{R}$eading furnishes the mind only with materials of knowledge; it is thinking makes what we read ours. We are of the ruminating kind, and it is not enough to cram ourselves with a great load of collections; unless we chew them over again they will not give us strength and nourishment.

JOHN LOCKE, *Of the Conduct of the Understanding* (1706)

$\mathbf{I}$t is one thing to own a library; another to use it wisely.

SIR JOHN LUBBOCK, *The Pleasures of Life* (1887)

$\mathbf{R}$eading does not make a man wise; it only makes him learned.

W. SOMERSET MAUGHAM, *A Writer's Notebook* (1949)

$\mathbf{T}$hat is the test to which I have urged that all books must at last be brought; if they do not bear it, their doom is fixed. They may be light or heavy, the penny sheet or the vast folio; they may speak of things seen or unseen; of Science or Art; of what has been or what is to be; they may amuse us or weary us, flatter us or scorn us; if they do not assist to make us better and more substantial men, they are only providing fuel for a fire larger and more utterly destructive than that which consumed the Library of the Ptolemies.

FREDERICK DENISON MAURICE, *The Friendship of Books and Other Lectures* (1873)

The study of books is a languishing and feeble activity that gives no heat, whereas discussion teaches and exercises us at the same time.

MICHEL EYQUEM DE MONTAIGNE, "Of the Art of Discussion," *Essays* (1580) [See Anonymous Chinese Saying, p. 170, and Woodrow Wilson, p. 182]

In books I have traveled, not only to other worlds, but into my own. I learned who I was and who I wanted to be, what I might aspire to, and what I might dare to dream about my world and myself. More powerfully and persuasively than from the "shalt nots" of the Ten Commandments, I learned the difference between good and evil, right and wrong. One of my favorite childhood books, *A Wrinkle in Time,* described that evil, that wrong, existing in a different dimension from our own. But I felt that I, too, existed much of the time in a different dimension from everyone else I knew. There was waking and there was sleeping. And then there were books, a kind of parallel universe in which anything might happen and frequently did, a universe in which I might be a newcomer but was never really a stranger. My real, true world. My perfect island.

ANNA QUINDLEN, *How Reading Changed My Life* (1998)

Since everything that comes into the human mind enters through the gates of sense, man's first reason is a reason of sense—experience. It is this that serves as a foundation for the reason of the intelligence; our first teachers in natural philosophy are our feet, hands, and eyes. To substitute books for them does not teach us to reason, it teaches us to use the reason of others rather than our own; it teaches us to believe much and know little.

JEAN-JACQUES ROUSSEAU, *Emile; or, Treatise on Education* (1762)

To use books rightly, is to go to them for help; to appeal to them when our knowledge and power fail; to be led by them into wider sight and purer concentration than our own, and to receive from them the united sentence of the judges and councils of all time, against our solitary and unstable opinions.

JOHN RUSKIN

In reading, the mind is, in fact, only the playground of another's thoughts. So it comes about that if anyone spends almost the whole day reading, and by way of relaxation devotes the intervals to some thoughtless pastime, he gradually loses the capacity for thinking; just as the man who always rides, at last forgets how to walk. This is the case with many learned persons; they have read themselves stupid.

ARTHUR SCHOPENHAUER, "On Books and Reading," *The Art of Literature* (1818)

Language is the soul of intellect, and reading is the essential process by which that intellect is cultivated beyond the commonplace experiences of everyday life.

CHARLES SCRIBNER

People get nothing out of books but what they bring to them.

GEORGE BERNARD SHAW, in "Grand Old Boy," *George Bernard Shaw: His Life and Personality* by Hesketh Pearson (1963)

The sole substitute for an experience which we have not ourselves lived through is art and literature.

ALEXANDER SOLZHENITSYN, Nobel Lecture, 1972

[The individual of] robust and healthy intellect who gathers the harvest of literature into his barns, threshes the straw, winnows the grain, grinds it at his own mill, bakes it in his own oven . . . eats the true bread of knowledge.

ROBERT SOUTHEY, *The Doctor* (1834–1847)

A truly good book teaches me better than to read it. I must soon lay it down, and commence living on its hint. . . . What I began by reading, I must finish by acting.

HENRY DAVID THOREAU, *Journal* (1884)

Some covet to have libraries in their houses . . . only for show; as if they were only to furnish their rooms, and not their minds; if the only having of store of books were sufficient to improve a man, the stationers would have the advantage of all others; but certainly books were made for use, and not for ostentation; in vain do they boast of full libraries that are contented to live with empty heads.

SIR WILLIAM WALLER, *Divine Meditations upon Several Occasions* (1680)

𝕴 would never read a book if it were possible to talk half an hour with the man who wrote it.

WOODROW WILSON, advice to his students at Princeton [See Anonymous Chinese Saying, p. 170, and Michel Eyquem de Montaigne, p. 178]

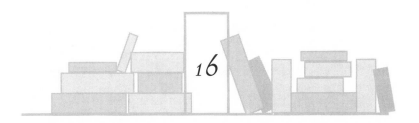

16

Authors and Their Readers

THE RELATIONSHIP BETWEEN authors and their
readers is a unique one, with the former, perhaps of
necessity, more aware of this uniqueness than the latter.
In what other circumstances do individuals reveal their
innermost thoughts, their deepest and darkest secrets,
to complete—albeit invisible—strangers?

Of course, authors and their readers want and
expect different things from this unique relationship.
Henry Wadsworth Longfellow spoke perhaps for all
authors when he said, "What a writer asks of his reader
is not so much to *like* as to *listen*." Conversely, looking
at it from the reader's perspective, Augustine Birrell
wrote, "Literature exists to please . . . and those men

of letters are the best loved who have best performed literature's truest office."

The one thing, however, that both writers and readers seem to agree on is that there *is* a relationship, and that both participants have a role to play in it, for good or ill. "Many books require no thought from those who read them," wrote Charles Caleb Colton, because "they made no such demand upon those who wrote them." On the other hand, as Ralph Waldo Emerson has written, "The profit of books is according to the sensibility of the reader; the profoundest thought or passion sleeps as in a mine, until it is discovered by an equal mind and heart."

The difference is slight, to the influence of an author, whether he is read by five hundred readers, or by five hundred thousand; if he can select the five hundred, he reaches the five hundred thousand.

HENRY ADAMS, *The Education of Henry Adams* (1907)

In relation to a writer, most readers believe in the Double Standard: they may be unfaithful to him as often as they like, but he must never, never be unfaithful to them.

W. H. AUDEN, "Reading," *The Dyer's Hand* (1962)

Why does the writing make us chase the writer? Why can't we leave well enough alone? Why aren't the books enough?

JULIAN BARNES, *Flaubert's Parrot* (1984)

I wouldn't mind writers so much if they didn't write books.

PETER BARNES, *Enchanted April* (screenplay) (1992)

It took me fifteen years to discover that I had no talent for writing, but I couldn't give it up because by that time I was too famous.

ROBERT BENCHLEY, in *Robert Benchley: A Biography* by Nathaniel Benchley (1955)

Of all the ways of acquiring books, writing them oneself is regarded as the most praiseworthy method.

WALTER BENJAMIN, "Unpacking My Library," *Illuminations* (1955)

A book chooses its readers as a play chooses its audience.

ALAN BENNETT, in *With Great Pleasure*, edited by Alec Reid (1986)

The theory these days (or one of them) is that the reader brings as much to the book as the author. So how much more do readers bring who have never managed to get through the book at all? It follows that the books one remembers best are the books one has never read.

ALAN BENNETT

It is strange how often men and women who write books forget all about the men and women who occasionally read them, a forgetful folly akin to that of the man who, having challenged a bruiser to engage in fisticuffs, lays down a plan of attack, but forgets to remember that his opponent is not likely to stand still all the time. Nowadays many readers are at least as clever as most authors.

AUGUSTINE BIRRELL, *Et Cetera* (1930)

Literature exists to please—to lighten the burden of men's lives; to make them for a short while forget their sorrow and their sins, their silenced hearths, their disappointed hopes, their grim futures—and those men of letters are the best loved who have best performed literature's truest office.

AUGUSTINE BIRRELL, "The Office of Literature," *The Collected Essays and Addresses* (1922)

A good reader is rarer than a good writer.

JORGE LUIS BORGES, in *The Dog Chairman*
by Robert Robinson (1982)

A conventional good read is usually a bad read, a
relaxing bath in what we know already. A true good read
is surely an act of innovative creation in which we, the
readers, become conspirators.

MALCOLM BRADBURY, in the *Sunday Times*,
November 29, 1987

What is responsible for the success of many works is
the rapport between the mediocrity of the author's ideas
and the mediocrity of the public's.

SÉBASTIAN-ROCH-NICOLAS CHAMFORT, *Maxims and
Thoughts* (1796) [See Charles Caleb Colton, p. 188, and
Horace Walpole, p. 193]

That writer does the most, who gives his reader the
most knowledge, and takes from him the least time.

CHARLES CALEB COLTON, *Lacon: or, Many Things in
Few Words; Addressed to Those Who Think* (1823)

Many books require no thought from those who read them, and for a very simple reason—they made no such demand upon those who wrote them.

CHARLES CALEB COLTON, *Lacon: or, Many Things in Few Words; Addressed to Those Who Think* (1823) [See Sébastian-Roch-Nicolas Chamfort, p. 187, and Horace Walpole, p. 193]

A great writer creates a world of his own and his readers are proud to live in it. A lesser writer may entice them in for a moment, but soon he will watch them filing out.

CYRIL CONNOLLY, *Enemies of Promise* (1938)

But who shall be the master, the writer or the reader?

DENIS DIDEROT, *Jacques le Fataliste* (1796)

There are no trashy writers—only trashy readers.

JULIUS J. EPSTEIN, *Reuben, Reuben* (screenplay) (1983)

He has gained every point who has mixed profit with pleasure, by delighting the reader at the same time as instructing him.

HORACE, *Ars Poetica* (c. 8 B.C.)

I do not read a book: I hold a conversation with the author.

ELBERT HUBBARD, *The Note Book of Elbert Hubbard,* compiled by Elbert Hubbard II (1927)

Sitting, last winter, among my books, and walled round with all the comfort and protection which they and my fireside could afford me; to wit, a table of high-piled books at my back, my writing-desk on one side of me, some shelves on the other, and the feelings of the warm fire at my feet; I began to consider how I loved the authors of those books: how I loved them, too, not only for the imaginative pleasures they afforded me, but for their making me love the very books themselves, and delight to be in contact with them.

LEIGH HUNT, *My Books* (1823)

One should never meet an artist whose work one admires. What he does is always so much better than what he is.

JOHN HUSTON AND ANTHONY VEILLER, *Moulin Rouge* (screenplay) (1952) [See Arthur Koestler, p. 190]

The privilege of adopting and adapting is one of the numerous benefactions conferred by writers upon readers, and every competent reader is tempted to re-write the book he is reading.

HOLBROOK JACKSON, *Bookman's Pleasure* (1945)

What is written without effort is in general read without pleasure.

DR. SAMUEL JOHNSON, in *Johnsonian Miscellanies* by Birkbeck Hill (1897)

A writer's ambition should be . . . to trade a hundred contemporary readers for ten readers in ten years' time and for one reader in a hundred years.

ARTHUR KOESTLER, in *The New York Times Book Review,* April 1, 1951

Liking a writer and then meeting the writer is like liking goose liver and then meeting the goose.

ARTHUR KOESTLER, in *The International Herald Tribune,* April 5, 1982 [See John Huston and Anthony Veiller, p. 189]

The words which are the writer's materials for expression are but the symbol of the ideas already existing in the mind of the reader.

VERNON LEE, *The Handling of Words and Other Studies in Literary Psychology* (1923)

What a writer asks of his reader is not so much to *like* as to *listen*.

HENRY WADSWORTH LONGFELLOW, in a letter to J. S. Dwight, December 10, 1847 [See George Orwell, below]

Make him [the reader] laugh and he will think you a trivial fellow, but bore him in the right way and your reputation is assured.

W. SOMERSET MAUGHAM, *The Gentleman in the Parlour* (1930)

When I sit down to write a book, I do not say to myself, "I am going to produce a work of art." I write it because there is some lie that I want to expose, some fact to which I want to draw attention, and my initial concern is to get a hearing.

GEORGE ORWELL, "Why I Write," *A Collection of Essays* (1954) [See Henry Wadsworth Longfellow, above]

What really knocks me out is a book that, when you're all done reading it, you wish the author that wrote it was a terrific friend of yours, and you could call him up on the phone whenever you felt like it.

J. D. SALINGER, *The Catcher in the Rye* (1951)

In reality, people read because they want to write. Anyway, reading is a sort of rewriting.

JEAN-PAUL SARTRE, *Between Existentialism and Marxism* (1974)

The man who writes for fools is always sure of a large audience.

ARTHUR SCHOPENHAUER, "On Books and Reading," *The Art of Literature* (1818)

To read a book in the true sense, to read it, that is, not as a critic but in the spirit of enjoyment—is to lay aside for the moment one's own personality and to become a part of the author.

LESLIE STEPHEN, *Hours in a Library* (1874)

Books have their fate from the capacities of their readers.

TERENTIANUS MAURUS, in *Maxims* by Thomas Wilson (1898)

Persons attempting to find a motive in this narrative will be prosecuted; persons attempting to find a moral

in it will be banished; persons attempting to find a plot in
it will be shot.

MARK TWAIN, "Notice," *The Adventures of Huckleberry
Finn* (1884)

I hope, reader, . . . we shall meet again. And we shall
recognize one another. And forgive me if I have troubled
you more than was needful and inevitable, more than I
intended to do when I took up my pen to distract you
for a while from your distractions. And may God deny
you peace, but give you glory!

MIGUEL DE UNAMUNO, *Tragic Sense of Life* (1913)

I am persuaded that foolish writers and readers are
created for each other; and that fortune provides readers
as she does mates for ugly women.

HORACE WALPOLE, August 17, 1773, *Letters of Horace
Walpole, Fourth Earl of Oxford,* edited by Peter Cunningham
(1891) [See Sébastian Roch Nicolas Chamfort, p. 187, and
Charles Caleb Colton, p. 188]

As in the sexual experience, there are never more than
two persons present in the act of reading—the writer

who is the impregnator, and the reader who is
the respondent.

E. B. WHITE, *The Second Tree from the Corner* (1954)

A writer can do nothing for men more necessary,
satisfying, than just simply to reveal to them the infinite
possibilities of their own souls.

WALT WHITMAN, in *With Walt Whitman in Camden*
by Horace Traubel (1908)

Camerado, this is no book,
Who touches this touches a man,
(Is it night? Are we here together alone?)
It is I you hold and who holds you.
I spring from the pages into your arms—decease calls
    me forth.

WALT WHITMAN, "So Long" (1881)

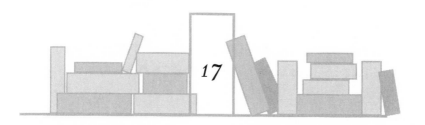

17

Collectors and Collecting

ONE OF THE MORE interesting aspects of the way
collectors view themselves is that they recognize and
readily admit that their collecting is a kind of illness,
albeit—as so many contend—a healthy illness. Some,
in fact, go so far as to argue that the desire to collect
is not only an illness but one that can be genetically
passed down to the next generation. In truth, there may
be something to this, as we know of many individuals
who, like their parents, are avid collectors of one sort
or another.

It is also true, however, that not everyone who
has a lot of books in his or her home is a collector in
the classic sense. That is, there are many among us who
have no particular interest in first editions, morocco

bindings, or presentation copies, and wouldn't be able to distinguish between foxing and chipping if our lives depended on it. In the end, though, such details are of little consequence for, like beauty, the value of any collection ultimately lies in the eye of the collector.

When people ask me, "Do you collect books?" I always say, "No, books collect me."

NICHOLAS BARKER, in *At Home with Books* by Estelle Ellis, Caroline Seebohm, and Christopher Simon Sykes (1995)

As a rule people don't collect books; they let books collect themselves.

ARNOLD BENNETT, *Things That Have Interested Me* (1926)

[There are no habits] more alien to the doctrine of the Communist than those of the collector, and there is no collector, not even the basest of them all, the Belial of his tribe, the man who collects money, whose sense of joys of ownership is keener than the book-collector's.

AUGUSTINE BIRRELL, *Collected Essays and Addresses* (1922)

To be proud of having two thousand books would be absurd. You might as well be proud of having two topcoats. After your first two thousand difficulty begins, but until you have ten thousand volumes the less you say about your library the better. *Then* you may begin to speak.

AUGUSTINE BIRRELL

Without disparaging the other forms of collecting, I confess a conviction that the human impulse to collect reaches one of its highest levels in the domain of books.

THEODORE C. BLEGEN

In the tight little cosmos of the fisher of books just one form of collecting is wholly admirable and understandable; namely, the acquisition of rare books and manuscripts. The book collector has known many stamp and coin collectors, old furniture men, old glass and old pewter men who turned to books, but he has never known a first-grade bookman who got down off his hobby before the undertaker was sent for.

BARTON W. CURRIE, *Fishers of Books* (1931)

Collectors and Collecting

Well, so far as I am concerned, he is the only collector who really matters . . . a man who loves books, and reads them. He loves books not only for what they have to say to him—though that is his principal reason—but for their look, their feel, yes, and even their smell. He is a man who may give books away, but who never thinks of buying a musty immortality with his library. His affair with books is a cheerful, life-enhancing passion.

ROBERTSON DAVIES, "Book Collecting" (1962),
The Enthusiasms of Robertson Davies, edited by Judith
Skelton Grant (1989)

In fact, the fame of our love of [books] had been soon winged abroad everywhere, and we were reported to burn with such desire for books, and especially old ones, that it was more easy for any man to gain our favour by means of books than of money.

RICHARD DE BURY, *Philobiblon* (1473)

O my darling books! A day will come when you will be laid out on the salesroom table, and others will buy and possess you—persons, perhaps, less worthy of you than your old master. Yet how dear to me are they all! Have I not chosen them one by one, gathered them in with the sweat of my brow? I do love you all!

SILVESTRE DE SACY

True collectors have, like lovers, an infinite sadness, even in their happiness. They know well that they can never put the world under lock and key in a glass case. Hence their profound melancholy.

ANATOLE FRANCE, "Bibliophilia," *On Life and Letters* (1914)

Book-collecting may have its quirks and eccentricities, but, on the whole, it is a vitalizing element in a society honeycombed by several sources of corruption.

WILLIAM GLADSTONE, in a letter to Bernard Quaritch, September 9, 1896

Bookmen, *men of letters,* students, and all manner of passionate readers are a species apart. . . . They become natives of a world of books, creatures of the printed word, and in the end cease to be men as, by gradual metastasis, they are resolved into bookmen: twice-born, first of woman (as every man) and then of books, and, by reason of this, unique and distinct from the rest.

HOLBROOK JACKSON

Some have been afflicted with bibliomania . . . from excess of affairs. Many . . . are so buried in the minor and immediate tasks of earning a living . . . whence it comes to pass that, slyly and insensibly perverted, nerves frayed and brains dulled, they take to books as sick souls take to drugs. They hoard at first against a time of leisure when they may perchance read, and end by hoarding for the sake of hoarding, thus allying themselves with those dizzards who wallow among possessions which they cannot use, and who die before they have lived.

HOLBROOK JACKSON, *The Anatomy of Bibliomania* (1930)

A presentation copy . . . is a copy of a book which does not sell, sent you by the author, with his foolish autograph at the beginning of it; for which, if a stranger, he only demands your friendship; if a brother author, he expects from you a book of yours, which does not sell, in return.

CHARLES LAMB, "Popular Fallacies," *Last Essays of Elia* (1833)

Book-collecting ought not to be a mere trade, or a mere fad; its object is to secure the comforts of home for examples really rare or beautiful, or interesting as relics.

ANDREW LANG, *Books and Bookmen* (1886)

It is because the passion for books is a sentimental passion that people who have not felt it always fail to understand it.

ANDREW LANG, "Bibliomania in France," *Books and Bookmen* (1886)

The fact that a book is in the public library brings no comfort. Books are the one element in which I am personally and nakedly acquisitive. If it weren't for the law I would steal them. If it weren't for my purse I would buy them.

HAROLD LASKI

The book-collector is the hermaphrodite of literature: neither a reader nor a writer.

SHANE LESLIE

A book's first life, it is true, depends upon its contents, but two or three years after publication the pagination, the print, the paper, the cover, and the shape of the book begin to attract, and year by year they attract more and more until the book attains the glory of a Chinese vase in which there is nothing but a little dust.

GEORGE MOORE, *Impressions and Opinions* (1913)

$\mathbb{A}$ man either collects books for his own intellectual profit, which is sane, or out of pure ostentatious vanity.

WILLIAM ROBERTS, *The Book-Hunter in London* (1895)

$\mathbf{A}$fter love, book collecting is the most exhilarating sport of all.

A. S. W. ROSENBACH

Book-collectors are buzzards who stretch their wings in anticipation as they wait patiently for a colleague's demise; and then they swoop down and ghoulishly grab some long-coveted treasure from the dear departed's trove.

A. S. W. ROSENBACH, *Books and Bidders* (1927)

$\mathfrak{I}$ suppose there are people—I've been told there are intelligent people—who would just as soon have an edition of Keats's *Poems,* for example, well printed on good paper, in a handsome modern binding, as a first edition in its original boards! I hope I shall never meet them.

A. S. W. ROSENBACH, *Books and Bidders* (1927)

You can't want to be a collector, you're born that way. Driven. It requires a mixture of ego, philanthropy, intellectual curiosity, excitement for the quest, and a genetic mutation toward the act of collecting itself.

MARVIN SACKNER, in *At Home with Books* by Estelle Ellis, Caroline Seebohm, and Christopher Simon Sykes (1995)

In nature the bird who gets up the earliest catches the most worms, but in book-collecting the prizes fall to birds who know worms when they see them.

MICHAEL SADLEIR, in *The Colophon,* Number 3, 1930

The great collections are vast, not complete. Incomplete: motivated by the desire for completeness. There is always one more. And even if you have everything—whatever that might be—then you will perhaps want a better copy (version, edition) of what you have; or with mass-produced objects (pottery, books, artifacts), simply an extra copy, in case the one you possess is lost or stolen or broken or damaged. A backup copy. A shadow collection. A great private collection is a material concentrate that continually stimulates, that overexcites. Not only because it can always be added to, but because it is already too much.

The collector's need is precisely for excess, for surfeit, for profusion.

It's too much—and it's just enough for me. Someone who hesitates, who asks, Do I need this? Is this really necessary? is not a collector. A collection is always more than is necessary.

SUSAN SONTAG, *The Volcano Lover* (1992)

When we are collecting books, we are collecting happiness.

VINCENT STARRETT

Behind all the paraphernalia of bibliography, behind the bookshops, auctions, exhibitions, catalogues, collations and research which define the collector's efforts, is the single fact of the love of books.

A.J.A. SYMONS, "The Book-Collector's Apology," *Book-Collectors Quarterly*

[No one can be] an orthodox collector or a true bibliophile who had not at one time committed a great and foolish extravagance.

DANIEL M. TREDWELL, *A Monograph on Privately Illustrated Books* (1892)

[Of all] impassioned pursuits, there is none more disturbing, more distressing in deception and hope, more intellectually absorbing, more obstinate in ill-success, more insatiable in triumph, more abundant in joys, noble, healthy and pure, than book-hunting.

OCTAVE UZANNE, *The Book-Hunter in Paris* (1893)

To turn over the pages of a book long coveted, to handle an unexpected find, to fondle a binding, to dust the edges, are exquisite joys in which the hand shares with the eye.

OCTAVE UZANNE, *The Book-Hunter in Paris* (1893)

In spite of folly, vulgarity and extravagance, the collecting of books is a pursuit for sane people. Its heart is sound, and its very blood is the record of man's achievement in the conquest of knowledge.

IOLO WILLIAMS, *The Elements of Book-Collecting* (1927)

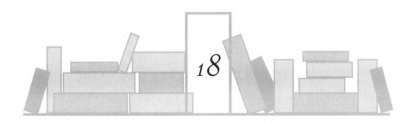

The Book Trade

THE BOOK TRADE—whether on the producing or on the selling side—is one that almost no one simply "falls into." Rather, people choose very consciously to enter the field, in most if not all cases because of a love of books, a love usually developed when they were children.

To the outsider publishing appears to be a glamorous, exciting, even romantic profession. And, in fact, it is all those things. But like any other field, it can also be dreary, boring, frustrating, and depressing. Moreover, it's an industry that always seems to be facing some crisis or another, whether it's the decreasing number of independent booksellers or the increasing number of people logging on to the Internet instead of reading books. And on top of all that, it pays poorly.

Even so, nearly everyone in the business loves it, and once they've entered it, there are few who leave it by choice. And the reason, no doubt, is because, despite the pitfalls, in the end it's still about books, and books are what they care about. For, as Geoffrey Faber once put it in an address to British booksellers, "Most of us would rather be making a competence out of books than a fortune out of soap."

First you have the writer who can write but can't spell. Then you have the editor who can spell but can't write. Finally you have the publisher who can neither spell nor write, and he makes all the money.

ANONYMOUS, in *Literary Agents: What They Do, How They Do It, and How to Find and Work with the Right One for You* by Michael Larsen (1996)

Editors are like the people who bought and sold in the book of Revelation; there is not one but has the mark of the beast upon him.

SAMUEL BUTLER

The theory is that if a famous author says another author is terrific, the public, sheeplike, will line up and buy the book in question.

WILLIAM COLE, on endorsements, *The New York Times Book Review*, July 23, 1978

University printing presses exist, and are subsidized by the Government for the purpose of producing books which no one can read; and they are true to their high calling.

FRANCIS M. CORNFORD, *Microcosmographia Academica* (1908)

A second-hand bookseller may belong to that unhappy class of men who have no belief in the good of what they get their living by, yet keep conscience enough to be morose rather than unctuous in their vocation.

GEORGE ELIOT, *Daniel Deronda* (1876)

For three years I was a managing director in a big brewery. I have no sort of quarrel with brewing. It is an admirable trade, and beer is an admirable drink. But I have never been so bored in my life as I was during those three years. I learned then the lesson that nothing is so depressing as to spend one's life doing something in which one is not interested. Most of us would rather be making a competence out of books than a fortune out of soap.

GEOFFREY FABER, in a speech to British booksellers, 1931, in *Ex Libris* by Christopher Morley (1936)

In today's [book] market, writers can't just be writers. They have to be performers and publicists as well. The image of the lonely writer honing his or her art is fast becoming outdated. What's demanded instead is something else: a hook, a smile and a shoeshine.

JOSHUA HENKIN, "Writer with a Roadshow," *The New York Times,* July 5, 1997

Editor: A person . . . whose business it is to separate the wheat from the chaff, and see that the chaff is printed.

ELBERT HUBBARD, *The Roycroft Dictionary Concocted by Ali Baba and the Bunch on Rainy Days* (1914)

The Foulis' editions of classical works were much praised by scholars and collectors in the nineteenth century. The celebrated Glasgow publishers once attempted to issue a book which should be a perfect specimen of typographical accuracy. Every precaution was taken to secure the desired result. Six experienced proof-readers were employed, who devoted hours to the reading of each page; and after it was thought to be perfect, it was posted up in the hall of the university, with a notification that a reward of fifty pounds would be paid to any person who could discover an error. Each page was suffered to remain two weeks in the place where it had been posted, before the work was printed, and the printers thought that they had attained the object for which they had been striving. When the work was issued, it was discovered that several errors had been committed, one of which was in the first line of the first page.

WILLIAM KEDDIE, *Anecdotes Literary and Scientific* (1894)

Intelligence and sympathy with literature has gone out of the [book publishing] trade almost wholly. I believe the general intelligence of the country has suffered from it.

ALEXANDER MACMILLAN, in a letter to William Gladstone, 1852, in *Dickens' Fur Coat and Charlotte's Unanswered Letters* by Daniel Pool (1997)

Though our publishers will tell you that they are ever seeking "original" writers, nothing could be farther from the truth. What they want is more of the same, only thinly disguised. They most certainly do not want another Faulkner, another Melville, another Thoreau, another Whitman. What the *public* wants, no one knows. Not even the publishers.

HENRY MILLER, "When I Reach for My Revolver" (1955)

The job of editor in a publishing house is the dullest, hardest, most exciting, exasperating, and rewarding of perhaps any job in the world.

MAXWELL PERKINS, *Editor to Author: The Letters of Maxwell Perkins,* edited by John Hall Wheelock (1950)

What we publishers think is that our function is to bring everything out into the open, on the theory that we have an adult population that knows values, or can learn them, and let them decide.

MAXWELL PERKINS, *Editor to Author: The Letters of Maxwell Perkins,* edited by John Hall Wheelock (1950)

The longest-lived editor is the one least distinguishable from his average reader.

ROBERT ROBINSON, *The Dog Chairman* (1982)

We are not a publisher; we are now a creator of copyrights for their exploitation in any medium or distribution system.

RICHARD SNYDER, speaking of Simon & Schuster, in *The New York Times*, June 30, 1991

The trouble with the publishing business is that too many people who have half a mind to write a book do so.

WILLIAM TARG, in "No Author Is a Man of Genius to His Publisher" by William Rossa Cole, *The New York Times Book Review*, September 3, 1989

As part of my research for *An Anthology of Author's Atrocity Stories About Publishers,* I conducted a study (employing my usual controls) that showed the average shelf life of a trade book to be somewhere between milk and yogurt.

CALVIN TRILLIN, *Uncivil Liberties* (1982)

Take an idiot man from a lunatic asylum and marry him to an idiot woman, and the fourth generation from this connection should be a good publisher from the American point of view.

MARK TWAIN

Publishers are not necessarily either philanthropists
or rogues. Likewise, they are usually neither lordly
magnates nor cringing beggars. As a working hypothesis,
regard them as ordinary human beings trying to earn
their living at an unusually difficult occupation.

SIR STANLEY UNWIN, *The Truth About Publishing* (1960)

Your book may be a masterpiece but do not suggest
that to the publisher because many of the most hopeless
manuscripts that have come his way have probably been
so described by their authors.

SIR STANLEY UNWIN, *The Truth About Publishing* (1960)

Our booksellers here at London disgrace literature by
the trash they bespeak to be written, and at the same
time prevent everything else from being sold. They are
little more or less than upholsterers, who sell *sets* or *bodies*
of arts and sciences for furniture; and the purchasers,
for I am very sure they are not readers, buy only in that
view. I never thought there was much merit in reading:
but yet it is too good a thing to be put upon no better
footing than damask and mahogany.

HORACE WALPOLE, in a letter to Sir David Dalrymple,
c. 1780

Editing is the most companionable form of education.

EDWARD WEEKS, *In Friendly Candor* (1959)

The bookseller who understands his business never shows any anxiety to sell his treasures; he acts as if it were a matter of perfect indifference to him whether he sells his books or not. His chief aim is to make his visitors feel at home in his shop, and having induced the customers to look at his wares, he leaves the books themselves to complete the transaction.

ROBERT M. WILLIAMSON, *Bits from an Old Bookshop* (1904)

The pleasure of benefiting humanity is a pleasure the bookseller possesses in no small degree. In purchasing books from people who are weary of them, or have no further use for them, he rescues literature from lying idly aside, or from being destroyed by moths or damp; and in re-selling these books to fresh readers, he gives forgotten authors a new lease of life, helps to keep the immortal spirit of learning alive, and gives anew to men the delights of knowing the great minds of the past.

ROBERT M. WILLIAMSON, *Bits from an Old Bookshop* (1904)

I'm not saying all publishers have to be literary, but some interest in books would help.

A. N. WILSON, in *Bookseller,* July 5, 1996

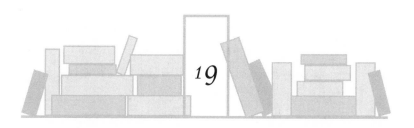

The Enemies of Books

BOOKS HAVE NOT ONLY a long history but also, unfortunately, a long history of enemies, both natural and otherwise. Among the former are bookworms and other vermin, fire, water, gas, heat, light, and dust. Due to their nature, such enemies are insidious rather than openly hostile, but dealing with them is more often than not simply a matter of care, and easy enough to accomplish if one has a mind to.

The other kind of enemies, however, are usually not only openly hostile but proudly so, and are considerably more difficult to deal with. These are the human enemies of books, those who believe they are entitled to decide what we should all think, recognize that the ability to read freely inevitably leads to the ability to think freely, and accordingly would keep books of which they don't approve out of our hands.

From the church's efforts to keep Galileo from publishing his findings in the seventeenth century, to the Nazi's book burnings of the 1930s, to the *fatwa* declared against Salman Rushdie in the 1980s, to the ongoing efforts to ban such American classics as *Huckleberry Finn*, those who would restrict our freedoms continue to make their presence felt. We might accordingly all be well advised to keep in mind Franklin D. Roosevelt's advice that "books are weapons. And it is a part of your dedication always to make them weapons for man's freedom."

You don't have to burn books to destroy a culture. Just get people to stop reading them.

RAY BRADBURY, in *Reader's Digest,* January 1994

Through and through th' inspired leaves,
Ye maggots, make your windings;
But, oh! respect his lordship's taste,
And spare his golden bindings.

ROBERT BURNS, "The Bookworms" (c. 1790)

Books are not good fuel. . . . In the days when heretical books were burned, it was necessary to place them on large wooden stages, and after all the pains were taken to demolish them, considerable readable masses were sometimes found in the embers; whence it was supposed that the devil, conversant in fire and its effects, gave them his special protection. In the end it was found easier and cheaper to burn the heretics themselves than their books.

JOHN HILL BURTON, *The Book-Hunter* (1862)
[See Heinrich Heine, p. 220]

Try to avoid your house catching fire, as this does no good at all. And while your house is still intact, it is a sound idea to persuade all babies and animals to live in another one—and if you really value your books, only offer hospitality to illiterates who won't persist in bloody touching them all the time. Mind you, you will have to tolerate them telling you you could open a shop with all these books (people have suggested this to me—in the shop) and betting that you haven't read them all.

JOSEPH CONNOLLY, *Modern First Editions* (1984)

Books are the curse of the human race. Nine-tenths of existing books are nonsense, and the clever books are the refutation of that nonsense. The greatest misfortune that ever befell man was the invention of printing.

BENJAMIN DISRAELI

Every burned book or house enlightens the world.

RALPH WALDO EMERSON

I don't like to read books; they muss up my mind.

HENRY FORD, in *The Hero in America: A Chronicle of Hero-Worship* by Dixon Wecter (1941)

What progress we are making. In the Middle Ages they would have burned me; nowadays they are content with burning my books.

SIGMUND FREUD, soon after the Nazis came to power in Germany, in *The Life and Work of Sigmund Freud* by Ernest Jones (1953–1957)

Wherever they burn books they will also, in the end, burn human beings.

HEINRICH HEINE, *Almansor: A Tragedy* (1823)
[See John Hill Burton, p. 219]

Speaking of Books

The author of the *Satanic Verses* book, which is against Islam, the Prophet, and the Koran, and all those involved in its publication who were aware of its contents, are sentenced to death. I ask all Moslems to execute them wherever they find them.

AYATOLLA RUHOLLA KHOMEINI, *Fatwa* against Salman Rushdie, February 14, 1989 [See John Mortimer, p. 222, and Salman Rushdie, p. 224]

The world is fundamentally hostile to literature, in great part because the world is gregarious, and literature is a solitary pursuit.

ANDREW LANG, in *The Pleasures of Bookland* by Joseph Shaylor (1910)

The crime of book purging is that it involves a rejection of the word. For the word is never absolute truth, but only man's frail and human effort to approach the truth. To reject the word is to reject the human search.

MAX LERNER, in the *New York Post*, June 24, 1953

The multitude of books is a great evil. There is no measure or limit to this fever for writing; every one must be an author; some out of vanity, to acquire celebrity and raise up a name; others for the sake of mere gain.

MARTIN LUTHER

To read too many books is harmful.

MAO TSE‑TUNG, in *The New Yorker,* March 7, 1977

Hell must be a place where you are only allowed to read what you agree with.

JOHN MORTIMER, in regard to the furor over Salman Rushdie's *The Satanic Verses,* the *Times,* March 5, 1989 [See Ayatolla Ruholla Khomeini, p. 221, and Salman Rushdie, p. 224]

I suppose that writers should, in a way, feel flattered by the censorship laws. They show a primitive fear and dread at the fearful magic of print.

JOHN MORTIMER, *Clinging to the Wreckage* (1982)

I have a low opinion of books; they are but piles of stones set up to show coming travelers where other minds have been. . . . One day's exposure to mountains is better than cartloads of books.

JOHN MUIR, in "The Philosophy of John Muir,"
The Wilderness World of John Muir, compiled by
Edwin Way Teale (1954)

The weapon of the dictator is not so much propaganda as censorship.

TERENCE H. QUALTER, *Propaganda and Psychological Warfare* (1962)

There is no one thing to be found in books which it is a disgrace not to know.

SIR WALTER RALEIGH

Books may be burned and cities sacked, but truth, like the yearning for freedom, lives in the hearts of humble men.

FRANKLIN D. ROOSEVELT, in his acceptance speech at the Democratic Party National Convention, June 27, 1936

We all know that books burn—yet we have the greater knowledge that books cannot be killed by fire. People die, but books never die. No man and no force can abolish memory. . . . In this war, we know, books are weapons. And it is a part of your dedication always to make them weapons for man's freedom.

FRANKLIN D. ROOSEVELT, in a message to the American Booksellers Association, May 6, 1942, in *Publishers Weekly*, May 9, 1942

To burn a book is not to destroy it. One minute of darkness will not make us blind.

SALMAN RUSHDIE, the *Weekend Guardian*, October 14–15, 1989 [See Ayatolla Ruholla Khomeini, p. 221, and John Mortimer, p. 222]

Woe to that nation whose literature is cut short by the intrusion of force. This is not merely interference with freedom of the press but the sealing up of a nation's heart, the excision of its memory.

ALEXANDER SOLZHENITSYN, in *Time*, February 25, 1974

Particularly against books the Home Secretary is. If we can't stamp out literature in the country, we can at least stop it being brought in from outside.

EVELYN WAUGH, *Vile Bodies* (1930)

God forbid that any book should be banned. The practice is as indefensible as infanticide.

REBECCA WEST, "The Tosh Horse,"
The Strange Necessity (1928)

To admit authorities, however heavily furred and gowned, into our libraries and let them tell us how to read, what to read, what value to place upon what we read, is to destroy the spirit of freedom which is the breath of those sanctuaries. Everywhere else we may be bound by laws and conventions—there we have none.

VIRGINIA WOOLF, *The Second Common Reader* (1932)

The Enemies of Books

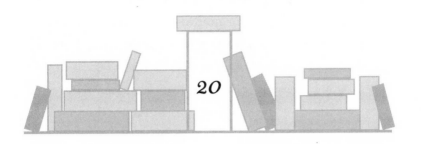

20

Books Forever!

BOOKS AS WE NOW think of them—that is, bundles of paper on which words are printed, bound together, and covered with either cloth or cardboard—have been in existence for something over half a millennium. In those five hundred years or so, they have changed the world more profoundly than any innovation before and, arguably, even since. They have also, perhaps as a result, become something akin to fetishes for some—if not many—devotees, even to the extent that they sometimes seem to be credited with almost supernatural powers.

The question for the future, of course, is whether or not there will continue to be books, either as we now think of them or otherwise. It may be that despite whatever technological innovations come, five hundred years from now there will still be individuals who wish to have bound bundles of printed paper on their shelves, and producers who are willing to accommodate them. On the other hand, it may be that, as was suggested in a recent advertisement for a soon-to-be-released Microsoft product, what we mean when we use the word *book* may change.

The answer is still far from clear, but ultimately it doesn't matter. For whether we continue to treasure those objects we now know as books, or at some point in the future find ourselves prizing something else we call by the same name, or even by some other name, we will always have a need for them, and in a sense they will always be there.

———

I took a speed-reading course where you run your finger down the middle of the page and was able to read *War and Peace* in twenty minutes. It's about Russia.

WOODY ALLEN, in a letter by Phyllis Mindell to *The New York Times*, September 3, 1995

Whose *Catcher in the Rye* is this? . . . You know, you wrote your name in all my books 'cause you knew this day was gonna come.

WOODY ALLEN AND MARSHALL BRICKMAN, *Annie Hall* (screenplay) (1977), Alvy Singer (Woody Allen) to Annie Hall (Diane Keaton) as they are ending their relationship and sorting out their books [See Nora Ephron, p. 233]

I remember when I was a little boy I once stole a pornographic book that was printed in Braille. And I used to rub the dirty parts.

WOODY ALLEN AND MICKEY ROSE, *Bananas* (screenplay) (1971)

O Lord, send the virtue of thy Holy Spirit upon these our books; that cleansing them from all earthly things, by thy holy blessing, they may mercifully enlighten our hearts and give us true understanding; and grant that by thy teaching, they may brightly preserve and make full an abundance of good works according to thy will.

ANONYMOUS PRAYER FROM A MEDIEVAL MONASTERY

Tell me what you read and I shall tell you what you are.

ANONYMOUS PROVERB

Books Forever!

My library shelves are the avenues of time.

ARCHBISHOP OF POITIERS, C. 1100

Americans like fat books and thin women.

RUSSELL BAKER

Fitting people with books is about as difficult as fitting them with shoes.

SYLVIA BEACH, *Shakespeare and Company* (1959)

When a writer dies, he becomes his books.

JORGE LUIS BORGES, *Labyrinths* (1962)

The contents of someone's bookcase are part of his history, like an ancestral portrait.

ANATOLE BROYARD, in *A Book Lover's Diary; The Reader's Companion* by Shelagh Wallace (1996)

The oldest books are only just out to those who have not read them.

SAMUEL BUTLER, *Further Extracts from the Note-Books of Samuel Butler,* edited by A. T. Bartholomew (1934)

Speaking of Books

I suppose there never was a man who had had so much to do with books as I have, who owned so few. I never have purchased a book which I could do without, or which I did not mean to read through.

THOMAS CARLYLE, *Letters,* edited by
Charles Eliot Norton (1888)

O thou who art able to write a Book . . . envy not him whom they name City⸗builder, and inexpressibly pity him whom they name Conqueror or City⸗burner! Thou too art a Conqueror and Victor; but of the true sort, namely over the Devil; thou too hast built what will outlast all marble and metal, and be a wonder⸗bringing City of the mind, a Temple and Seminary, and Prophetic Mount, whereto all kindreds of the earth will pilgrim.

THOMAS CARLYLE, *Sartor Resartus* (1838)

"What is the use of a book," thought Alice, "without pictures or conversations?"

LEWIS CARROLL, *Alice's Adventures in Wonderland* (1865)

The original writer is not one who imitates nobody, but one whom nobody can imitate.

FRANÇOIS RENÉ DE CHATEAUBRIAND, *Le Génie du Christianisme* (1802)

There is a great deal of difference between the eager man who wants to read a book, and the tired man who wants a book to read.

G. K. CHESTERTON, *Charles Dickens* (1906)

For lovers of books . . . a house without books is no house at all; and in a family where books make a great part of the pleasure of living, they must be where they can be got at without trouble, and what is of more importance, where they can share in the life about them and receive some touches of the humanity they supply and feed.

CLARENCE COOK, *The House Beautiful* (1878)

It is altogether befitting the decency of a scholar that washing should without fail precede reading, as often as he returns from his meals to study, before his fingers, besmeared with grease, loosen a clasp or turn over the leaf of a book.

RICHARD DE BURY, *Philobiblon* (1473)

Of making many books there is no end; and much study is a weariness of the flesh.

ECCLESIASTES 12:12

I do then with my friends as I do with my books. I would have them where I can find them, but I seldom use them.

RALPH WALDO EMERSON, "Friendship,"
Essays: First Series (1841)

Meek young men grow up in libraries, believing it their duty to accept the views which Cicero, which Locke, which Bacon, have given, forgetful that Cicero, Locke and Bacon were only young men in libraries, when they wrote these books.

RALPH WALDO EMERSON, *The American Scholar* (1837)

Men over forty are no judges of a book written in a new spirit.

RALPH WALDO EMERSON, "The Man of Letters,"
Lectures and Biographical Sketches (1883)

Put your name in your books now while you're unpacking them, before they get all mixed up together and you can't remember whose is whose.

NORA EPHRON, *When Harry Met Sally* (screenplay) (1989), Harry Burns (Billy Crystal) advises his friends (Carrie Fisher and Bruno Kirby) to prepare for a future breakup even as they move in together [See Woody Allen and Marshall Brickman, p. 229]

Books Forever!

Read much, but not many Books.

BENJAMIN FRANKLIN, *Poor Richard's Almanack*, February 1738

The Body of Benjamin Franklin, Printer (like the cover of an old book, its contents torn out, and stripped of its lettering and gilding), lies here, food for worms; but the work shall not be lost, for it will (as he believed) appear once more in a new and more elegant edition, revised and corrected by the Author.

BENJAMIN FRANKLIN, epitaph on himself, 1728

I've been in love three hundred times in my life, and all but five were with books.

LEE GLICKSTEIN

[Books are] the furniture of the mind.

SIR EDMUND GOSSE, *The Library of Edmund Gosse* (1924)

Books are like works of art. You enjoy them, you're their guardian for a while, you're aware that other people have owned and enjoyed them for a short time, and then they are passed on.

ERVIN HARRIS, in *At Home with Books* by Estelle Ellis, Caroline Seebohm, and Christopher Simon Sykes (1995)

Speaking of Books

One would imagine that books were, like women, the worse for being old; that they have a pleasure in being read for the first time; that they open their leaves more cordially; that the spirit of enjoyment wears out with the spirit of novelty; and that, after a certain age, it is high time to put them on the shelf.

WILLIAM HAZLITT, "On Reading New Books," *Sketches and Essays* (1839) [See "Mrs. William Hazlitt," below]

One could say that men are, like bookmarks, the worse for being old. They have a certain pleasure of being new—freshly picked up at the book shop or library; crisply stiff, standing proudly at attention marking their place within one's pages. The spirit of enjoyment and utility wears out with the spirit of novelty as the edges fray, and time and usage impart their limpening legacy. After a certain age, what can a woman do with such a thing? Abandon it to the dustbin or some lonely shelf? Heavens no. We simply turn down the corner of the page, and tuck the beloved old bookmark somewhere between the leaves, where it belongs.

"MRS. WILLIAM HAZLITT" (aka Jennifer Brehl), "On Bookmarks I Have Known" (2000) [See William Hazlitt, above]

I always believed in life rather than books.

OLIVER WENDELL HOLMES, SR., *The Autocrat at the Breakfast-Table* (1858) [See Logan Pearsall Smith, p. 242, and Robert Louis Stevenson, p. 242]

The first thing, naturally, when one enters a scholar's study or library, is to look at his books. One gets a notion very speedily of his tastes and the range of his pursuits by a glance round his bookshelves.

OLIVER WENDELL HOLMES, SR., *The Poet at the Breakfast-Table* (1872)

This will never be a civilized country until we expend more money for books than we do for chewing gum.

ELBERT HUBBARD, in *The Philistine*, 1895–1915

The proper study of mankind is books.

ALDOUS HUXLEY, *Crome Yellow* (1921)

Books are the cosmography of man, a world in themselves.

HOLBROOK JACKSON, *The Anatomy of Bibliomania* (1930)

Book-love, I say again, lasts throughout life, it never flags or fails, but, like Beauty itself, is *a joy for ever*.

HOLBROOK JACKSON, *The Anatomy of Bibliomania* (1930)

Never put off till to-morrow the book you can read today.

HOLBROOK JACKSON, *The Anatomy of Bibliomania* (1930)

No, sir, do *you* read books *through?*

DR. SAMUEL JOHNSON, on being asked if he had read a new book through, in *The Life of Samuel Johnson* by James Boswell (1791)

People in general do not willingly read, if they can have any thing else to amuse them.

DR. SAMUEL JOHNSON, in *The Life of Samuel Johnson* by James Boswell (1791)

Dictionaries are like watches, the worst is better than none, and the best cannot be expected to go quite true.

DR. SAMUEL JOHNSON, in a letter to Francesco Sastres, in *The Life of Samuel Johnson* by James Boswell (1791)

When I would know thee, Goodyere, my thought looks
Upon thy well-made choice of friends and books;
Then do I love thee, and behold thy ends
In making thy friends books, and thy books friends.

BEN JONSON

The books we plan to read in our old age are something like the places where we should wish to grow old.

LAURENT JOUBERT, *Selected Thoughts* (c. 1580)

Books are a narcotic.

FRANZ KAFKA, in *Conversations with Kafka* by Gustav Janouch (1953)

With a binding like you've got, people are going to want to know what's in the book.

ALAN JAY LERNER, *An American in Paris* (screenplay) (1951), spoken by Gene Kelly to Leslie Caron

My best friend is a person who will give me a book I have not read.

ABRAHAM LINCOLN

Outside of a dog, a book is man's best friend; inside of a dog, it's too dark to read.

GROUCHO MARX

Let our books have some of the qualities of music. But they must be the qualities that music has for the unmusical, what we want are dreams, and sound without sense.

HOPE MIRRLEES, "Bedside Books," *Life and Letters* (1928)

It is more of a job to interpret the interpretations than to interpret the things, and there are more books about books than about any other subject: we do nothing but write glosses about each other.

MICHEL EYQUEM DE MONTAIGNE, *Essays* (1580)

There are some books which cannot be adequately reviewed for twenty or thirty years after they come out.

JOHN, VISCOUNT MORLEY OF BLACKBURN, *Recollections* (1917)

Never let it be said that you allowed a book about books to usurp the power of the books themselves.

DANIEL J. O'NEILL

Books Forever!

A book in itself is always something more than paper and type and binder's boards. It possesses a subtle friendliness that sets it apart from other inanimate objects about us, and stamps it with an individuality which responds to our approach in proportion to our interest.

WILLIAM DANA ORCUTT

Literature is doomed if liberty of thought perishes.

GEORGE ORWELL, "The Prevention of Literature," *The Collected Essays, Journalism and Letters of George Orwell,* edited by Sonia Orwell and Ian Angus (1968)

I would hardly go so far as to say that a book without an autograph, a bookplate, a thumb mark, a marginal note, a dog-ear, a slightly (but only slightly, please!) broken back, is but half a book. Yet there is something to be said for the notion that a book fresh from the press or the publisher's shelf is like a feast uneaten, a wine untasted, a colt unbroken, a talent unused. Such a book is too virginal for any but a furtive and frigid bibliotaph. For me, I prefer "good, second-hand condition"—with preferably a few stains of varied sorts, and a scribbled comment or two by a learned or ribald owner. Such a

book has at some time found a friend and been
welcomed to someone's hearth.

CARL PURINGTON ROLLINS

You can't tell a book by its movie.

LOUIS A. SAFIAN, *The Book of Updated Proverbs* (1967)

All the same, [books] do serve some purpose. Culture
doesn't save anything or anyone, it doesn't justify. But
it's a product of man: he projects himself into it, he
recognizes himself in it; that critical mirror alone offers
him his image.

JEAN PAUL SARTRE, *Les Mots* (1964)

Everything in the world exists in order that it may end
up in a book.

RANDALL SHORT, in *The New York Times*,
January 27, 1991

For I bless God in the libraries of the learned and for
all the booksellers in the world.

CHRISTOPHER SMART, *Jubilate Agno* (1763)

Books Forever!

People say that life is the thing, but I prefer reading.

LOGAN PEARSALL SMITH, *Afterthoughts* (1931)
[See Oliver Wendell Holmes, Sr., p. 235, and Robert Louis
Stevenson, below]

[There is] no furniture so charming as books, even if
you never open them, or read a single word.

SYDNEY SMITH, in *A Memoir of the Reverend Sydney Smith*
by Lady Holland (1855)

I never read a book before reviewing it; it prejudices
a man so.

SYDNEY SMITH, in *The Smith of Smiths*
by Hesketh Pearson (1934)

Books are good enough in their own way, but they are
a mighty bloodless substitute for life.

ROBERT LOUIS STEVENSON, "An Apology for Idlers,"
Virginibus Puerisque (1881) [See Oliver Wendell Holmes, Sr.,
p. 235, and Logan Pearsall Smith, above]

Every book is, in an intimate sense, a circular letter to
the friends of him who writes it.

ROBERT LOUIS STEVENSON

Books, like proverbs, receive their chief value from the stamp and esteem of ages through which they have passed.

SIR WILLIAM TEMPLE, "Ancient and Modern Learning," *Miscellanea* (1690)

There are no race of people who talk about books, or perhaps, who read books, so little as literary men.

WILLIAM MAKEPEACE THACKERAY

Education . . . has produced a vast population able to read but unable to distinguish what is worth reading.

GEORGE MACAULAY TREVELYAN, *English Social History* (1942)

I like a thin book because it will steady a table, a leather volume because it will strop a razor, and a heavy book because it can be thrown at a cat.

MARK TWAIN

The man who does not read good books has no advantage over the man who can't read them.

MARK TWAIN

No girl was ever ruined by a book.

JAMES J. WALKER, Mayor of New York

If the books which you read are your own, mark with
a pen or pencil the most considerable things in them
which you desire to remember. Then you may read that
book the second time over with half the trouble, by
your eye running over the paragraphs which your pencil
has noted. It is but a very weak objection against this
practice to say, "I shall spoil my book"; for I persuade
myself that you did not buy it as a bookseller, to sell
again for gain, but as a scholar, to improve your mind
by it; and if the mind be improved, your advantage is
abundant, though your book yields less money to
your executors.

ISAAC WATTS, *Logic, On the Right Use of Reason in the
Enquiry after Truth* (1724)

Speaking of Books

Index of Authors

Abrahams, Israel, 18
Adams, Henry, 184
Adams, J. Donald, 140
Addison, Joseph, 4, 68
Aiken, John, 4
Alcott, A. Bronson, 126, 140
Alcott, Louisa May, 58
Allen, Woody, 228
Allen, Woody, and Marshall
  Brickman, 229
Allen, Woody, and Mickey
  Rose, 229
Anonymous, 19, 58, 98, 141, 152,
  208
Anonymous Chinese Saying,
  170
Anonymous Japanese Proverb,
  170
Anonymous Prayer, 229
Anonymous Proverb, 229
Archbishop of Poitiers, 230
Arnold, Matthew, 46
Aubrey, John, 170–171
Auchincloss, Louis, 58
Auden, W. H., 82, 126, 184
Austen, Jane, 162

Bacon, Francis, 5, 30, 82, 106, 114,
  141
Bagehot, Walter, 127
Baker, Russell, 230

Baldwin, James, 46
Balfour, Lord Arthur James,
  106, 114–115, 141
Barker, Nicholas, 196
Barnes, Julian, 83, 185
Barnes, Peter, 185
Barrie, James M., 47
Barrow, Isaac, 83, 141
Bartholin, Thomas V., 47
Barzini, Luigi, 115
Baxter, Richard, 30–31
Beach, Sylvia, 230
Beattie, James, 47, 68
Beecher, Henry Ward, 5, 19, 59,
  115, 162
Belloc, Hilaire, 163
Benchley, Robert, 185
Benjamin, Walter, 153, 185
Bennett, Alan, 127, 185, 186
Bennett, Arnold, 127, 196
Bennett, Jessie Lee, 83
Bennoch, Francis, 20
Bernard, Saint, 171
Bierce, Ambrose, 127
Birrell, Augustine, 20, 31, 142,
  186, 196, 197
Blegen, Theodore C., 197
Blessington, Lady Marguerite,
  128
Bloom, Allan, 83
Bohatta, Hanns, 59

Bologna, Joseph, David Zelag
    Goodman, and Renee
    Taylor, 83–84
Boorstin, Daniel J., 47–48
Borges, Jorge Luis, 116, 187, 230
Bradbury, Malcolm, 187
Bradbury, Ray, 218
Browning, Elizabeth Barrett,
    6, 107
Broyard, Anatole, 230
Brydges, Sir Samuel Egerton,
    68
Bulwer-Lytton, Edward, 31, 48, 171
Burden, Carter, 98
Burgess, Anthony, 20, 48
Burke, Edmund, 171
Burns, Robert, 218
Burton, John Hill, 20–21, 99, 219
Burton, Robert, 142
Butler, Samuel, 84, 208, 230
Byatt, A. S., 48
Byron, George Gordon, Lord,
    69

Calvino, Italo, 107, 128
Carlyle, Thomas, 6, 7, 49,
    171–172, 231
Carrel, Alexis, 116
Carroll, Lewis, 231
Cervantes Saavedra, Miguel
    de, 128
Chamfort, Sébastian-Roch-
    Nicolas, 128, 172, 187
Chandos, Grey Brydges, Lord,
    172–173
Channing, William Ellery, 7, 31,
    49, 84–85

Chateaubriand, François René
    de, 85, 231
Chesterfield, Philip Dormer
    Stanhope, Earl of, 32, 69, 99,
    173
Chesterton, G. K., 33, 129, 232
Churchill, Winston S., 21, 33
Cicero, 7, 21, 142
Clinton, William Jefferson, 49
Cole, William, 209
Coleridge, Hartley, 129
Coleridge, Samuel Taylor, 33
Collier, Jeremy, 143, 173, 174
Collins, William, 129
Colton, Charles Caleb, 33, 85,
    174, 187, 188
Connolly, Cyril, 129, 130, 188
Connolly, Joseph, 219
Conrad, Joseph, 7
Cook, Clarence, 232
Cook, Sir Edward, 130
Cornford, Francis M., 209
Cowley, Abraham, 22
Crabbe, George, 116, 174–175
Currie, Barton W., 22, 197

Davies, Robertson, 59–60, 107,
    108, 198
Davis, Thomas, 116
Dawson, George, 69, 116
De Bury, Richard, 8, 22, 86, 198,
    232
De Quincey, Thomas, 130, 175
De Sacy, Silvestre, 198
Descartes, René, 86
Dibdin, Thomas Frognall, 60, 143
Dickinson, Emily, 86, 130, 143

Diderot, Denis, 188
Disraeli, Benjamin, 34, 49–50,
    175, 219–220
D'Israeli, Isaac, 60–61, 153
Doner, Michele Oka, 100
Doyle, Arthur Conan, 144
Drummond, William, 117
Du Bois, H. P., 153
Dunbar, Maurice, 61
Duncan, David, 50

Ecclesiastes, 232
Eco, Umberto, 69
Eliot, Charles W., 87
Eliot, George, 209
Elliot, George P., 50
Emerson, Ralph Waldo, 34, 87,
    88, 117, 130, 131, 144, 176, 220,
    233
Ephron, Nora, 233
Epstein, Julius J., 188
Erasmus, Desiderius, 61

Faber, Geoffrey, 209–210
Fadiman, Clifton, 88
Ferrero, Guglielmo, 61
Ferriar, Dr. John, 61
Field, Eugene, 8, 23, 108, 144
Fitch, George Hamlin, 34–35, 145
FitzGerald, S. J. Adair, 62
Flaubert, Gustave, 88
Foot, Michael, 50
Ford, Ford Madox, 131
Ford, Henry, 220
Forster, E. M., 50–51, 131
France, Anatole, 62, 154, 199
Franklin, Benjamin, 234

Freud, Sigmund, 220
Froude, J. A., 35
Fuller, Thomas, 145, 176

Garrod, Heathcote William,
    145
Gibbon, Edward, 51
Gibbons, Kaye, 88
Gissing, George, 70, 146
Gladstone, William, 8, 199
Glickstein, Lee, 234
Godwin, William, 118
Golden, Harry, 89, 108
Goldsmith, Oliver, 35, 146
Gordon, Caroline, 70
Gordon, John Steele, 100
Gosse, Sir Edmund, 23, 234
Grade, Chaim, 100
Grass, Günter, 131
Grayson, David, 70
Greene, Graham, 163
Greer, Germaine, 118
Grey of Fallodon, Edward,
    Viscount, 70
Gruber, Frank, 9

Haliburton, Thomas Chandler,
    131
Hamerton, Philip Gilbert, 71
Hamill, Pete, 100–101
Hardwick, Elizabeth, 71
Hare, A. W. and J. C., 35, 89
Harington, Sir John, 176
Harris, Ervin, 234
Harrison, Frederic, 36, 62, 89
Hawthorne, Nathaniel, 108
Hayakawa, S. I., 71

Index of Authors

Hayes, Helen, 163
Hazlitt, William, 89, 163, 235
"Hazlitt, Mrs. William"
  (Jennifer Brehl), 235
Hearn, Lafcadio, 37–38, 154
Heath, D., 90
Heber, Richard, 63
Heine, Heinrich, 220
Heinsius, 118
Hemingway, Ernest, 131–132
Henkin, Joshua, 210
Herbert, George, 71
Herschel, Sir John Frederick
  William, 51, 72
Hersey, John, 90
Hesse, Hermann, 9
Hilton, James, 118–119
Hird, Frank, 154
Hobbes, Thomas, 132
Holmes, Oliver Wendell, Sr.,
  23, 51, 63, 101, 119, 235, 236
Holt, Henry, 101
Hood, Thomas, 90
Horace, 72, 188
Hubbard, Elbert, 176, 189, 210,
  236
Hubbard, Kin, 154
Hugo, Victor, 51–52
Humphrey, William, 90
Hunt, Leigh, 24, 90–91, 119, 146,
  155, 177, 189
Huston, John, and Anthony
  Veiller, 189
Huxley, Aldous, 109, 132, 236

Ibn Tibbon, Judah, 146–147
Irving, Washington, 147

Jackson, Holbrook, 9–10, 38, 52,
  63, 72, 91, 109, 132, 155, 164,
  189–190, 199–200, 236, 237
Jacobs, Ben, and Helena
  Hjalmarsson, 119–120
James I, King, 120
Jefferson, Thomas, 91
Johnson, Dr. Samuel, 39, 91–92,
  120, 147, 164, 165, 190, 237
Jonson, Ben, 237
Joubert, Laurent, 39, 238
Judah the Pious, Rabbi, 2

Kafka, Franz, 40, 238
Kazin, Alfred, 133
Keddie, William, 210–211
Keller, Helen, 148
Kempis, Thomas à, 73, 148
Kenko, Yoshida, 73
Khomeini, Ayatolla Ruholla,
  221
Koestler, Arthur, 190
Kraus, Karl, 109

Lamb, Charles, 24, 73, 92, 133,
  156, 200
Landor, Walter Savage, 73
Lang, Andrew, 92, 200, 201, 221
Langford, John Alfred, 10, 40
Laski, Harold, 201
Lawrence, Kathleen Rockwell,
  165
Lebowitz, Fran, 40
Lee, Harper, 74
Lee, Vernon, 190
Le Gallienne, Richard, 10–11,
  120

Lehmann-Haupt, Christopher, 133

Lerner, Alan Jay, 238

Lerner, Max, 221

Leslie, Shane, 201

Levenson, Sam, 165

Lewis, C. S., 165

Lichtenberg, Georg Christoph, 93

Lincoln, Abraham, 109, 238

Locke, John, 177

Lodge, Henry Cabot, 148

Logan, James, 63

London, Jack, 93

Longfellow, Henry Wadsworth, 148, 191

Lowell, Amy, 11, 93

Lowell, James Russell, 74, 121, 149

Lubbock, Sir John, 177

Luther, Martin, 221–222

Lyly, John, 64

Macaulay, Rose, 74

Macaulay, Thomas B., 74, 75, 121

MacLeish, Archibald, 121

Macmillan, Alexander, 211

Mansfield, Katherine, 75

Mao Tse-tung, 222

Marek, Richard, 64

Marx, Groucho, 238

Marx, Karl, 52

Mathias, T. J., 52

Maugham, W. Somerset, 40, 177, 191

Maurice, Frederick Denison, 177–178

Mawson, Timothy, 101

Melville, Herman, 93

Member of Parliament, 133

Mencken, H. L., 64, 134

Michell, John, 64

Miller, Henry, 134, 211–212

Milton, John, 11, 12, 110

Mirrlees, Hope, 239

Mitford, Nancy, 134

Mitterand, François, 93

Monkhouse, Cosmo, 65

Montagu, Lady Mary Wortley, 75

Montaigne, Michel Eyquem de, 24, 41, 149, 178, 239

Montesquieu, Charles de Secondat, Baron de la Brède et de, 149

Moore, George, 52, 201

Morley, Christopher, 94, 157

Morley of Blackburn, John, Viscount, 239

Mortimer, John, 222

Mouravit, Gustave, 65

Muir, John, 222–223

Neruda, Pablo, 65

Newton, A. Edward, 25

Nock, Albert Jay, 41

Norris, Kathleen, 149

O'Connor, Flannery, 134

O'Neill, Daniel J., 239

Orcutt, William Dana, 240

Orwell, George, 191, 240

Osborne, Francis, 41

Pater, Walter, 53

Payn, James, 149
Peacham, Henry, 101–102
Peacock, Thomas Love, 12, 135
Pepys, Samuel, 75
Perkins, Maxwell, 212
Petrarch, Francesco, 12–13, 25,
    65, 102
Phelps, Austin, 25
Phelps, William Lyon, 76
Phillipps, Sir Thomas, 102
Pliny, 94
Pliny the Younger, 150
Poe, Edgar Allan, 135
Postman, Neil, 165
Pound, Ezra, 136
Prescott, Peter S., 136
Proust, Marcel, 94, 166

Qualter, Terence H., 223
Quindlen, Anna, 53, 102, 166,
    178–179

Raabe, Tom, 66
Rabelais, François, 41
Raleigh, Sir Walter, 25, 223
Roberts, William, 94, 202
Robinson, Robert, 212
Rochman, Hazel, 76
Rollins, Carl Purington, 240–241
Roosevelt, Franklin D., 223–224
Roscommon, Wentworth
    Dillon, Earl of, 41
Rosenbach, A.S.W., 66, 202
Rosenblatt, Roger, 157–159, 166
Roth, Philip, 121
Rousseau, Jean-Jacques, 136, 179
Rowan, Carl, 122

Rushdie, Salman, 13, 95, 224
Ruskin, John, 26, 42, 95, 110,
    179–180
Russell, Lord John, 76

Sackner, Marvin, 203
Sadleir, Michael, 203
Safian, Louis A., 241
Sagan, Carl, 166
Sagan, Françoise, 103
Salinger, J. D., 191
Sartre, Jean-Paul, 192, 241
Schopenhauer, Arthur, 103, 110,
    136, 180, 192
Schwartz, Lynne Sharon, 76–77
Scott, Sir Walter, 150, 159
Scribner, Charles, 180
Seneca, 95, 103
Shakespeare, William, 122
Shaw, George Bernard, 53, 180
Sheffield, John, 137
Sherbrooke, Robert Lowe,
    Lord, 77
Sheridan, Thomas, 14
Short, Randall, 241
Singer, Isaac Bashevis, 167
Smart, Christopher, 241
Smith, Alexander, 122
Smith, Logan Pearsall, 78, 242
Smith, Sydney, 242
Snyder, Richard, 213
Solzhenitsyn, Alexander, 181,
    224
Sontag, Susan, 203–204
Southey, Robert, 26, 27, 66, 150,
    181
Starrett, Vincent, 204

Steele, Sir Richard, 78
Stein, Gertrude, 42
Stephen, Leslie, 192
Sterne, Laurence, 14
Stevenson, Robert Louis, 242
Stewart, Donald Ogden, 14
Styron, William, 95
Symons, A.J.A., 204
Szathmary, Louis, 103

Talbot, Catherine, 78
Targ, William, 27, 213
Temple, Sir William, 243
Terentianus Maurus, 192
Thackeray, William
    Makepeace, 123, 243
Thoreau, Henry David, 15, 42,
    53, 54, 111, 181
Thurber, James, 111
Tomlinson, H. M., 137
Tredwell, Daniel M., 204
Trevelyan, George Macaulay,
    243
Trillin, Calvin, 213
Trollope, Anthony, 78
Tuchman, Barbara, 54
Tupper, Martin Farquhar, 15
Twain, Mark, 192–193, 213, 243

Unamuno, Miguel de, 193
Unwin, Sir Stanley, 214
Uzanne, Octave, 205

Van Doren, Carl, 137
Van Gogh, Vincent, 15
Vass, Joan, 111
Vizinczey, Stephen, 96

Voltaire, 104

Walker, James J., 244
Walker, W., 112
Waller, Sir William, 181–182
Walpole, Horace, 193, 214
Watts, Isaac, 244
Waugh, Evelyn, 123, 224
Webster, Daniel, 54
Weeks, Edward, 215
Welty, Eudora, 167
Werfel, Franz, 27
West, Rebecca, 225
White, E. B., 193–194
Whitman, Walt, 112, 194
Wilde, Oscar, 55, 137
William IV, King, 55
Williams, Iolo, 205
Williamson, Robert M., 215
Wilson, A. N., 216
Wilson, Edmund, 96
Wilson, John, 112
Wilson, Woodrow, 182
Winchester, Caleb T., 138
Winfrey, Oprah, 167
Woolf, Virginia, 43, 79, 225
Wordsworth, William, 79

About the Editors

ROB KAPLAN has over twenty-five years' experience in the book publishing industry, having served in senior-level editorial positions with several major New York–based publishing houses before starting his own literary services firm, Rob Kaplan Associates, in 1998. His previous books include *A Passion for Books* (Times Books, 1999), which he co-edited with Mr. Rabinowitz, and *Science Says: A Collection of Quotations on the History, Meaning, and Practice of Science* (W. H. Freeman, 2000). He lives with his family in Cortlandt Manor, New York.

HAROLD RABINOWITZ was raised in the Williamsburg section of Brooklyn and attended yeshiva and rabbinical seminaries until the age of twenty-four, also earning graduate degrees in physics and philosophy along the way. He served as a congregational rabbi in Massachusetts for eight years before entering the world of publishing. He has served in senior editorial positions at Shenkman; Gordon and Breach; Grolier; and McGraw-Hill, and has been director of The Reference Works, a New York book packaging firm, since 1994. His translations of Yiddish fiction and poetry have been acclaimed in the United States and Israel. He is the author of many books on subjects as diverse as aviation and Jewish folklore. He and his wife, Ilana, and their son, Daniel, live in the Riverdale section of the Bronx.